MUSICIANS IN ANIMAL GUISE INCLUDE A DEER, AN ARMADILLO, A RABBIT. HEIGHT, 8 1/2 INCHES.

A YOUNG LORD PULLS AN UNDERWORLD GOD FROM A CONCH SHELL. HEIGHT, 5 3/4 INCHES.

To Syd :-

Hope you enjoy it

Love

Bill &

Marjory

Christmas   1977

By GEORGE E. STUART *and* GENE S. STUART
Photographs by DAVID ALAN HARVEY *and* OTIS IMBODEN
Prepared by the Special Publications Division
National Geographic Society, Washington, D.C.

The Mysterious MAYA

The Mysterious Maya

By George E. Stuart *and* Gene S. Stuart
Photographs by David Alan Harvey *and*
 Otis Imboden
Paintings by Louis S. Glanzman

Published by
The National Geographic Society
Robert E. Doyle, *President*
Melvin M. Payne, *Chairman of the Board*
Gilbert M. Grosvenor, *Editor*
Melville Bell Grosvenor, *Editor Emeritus*

Prepared by
The Special Publications Division
Robert L. Breeden, *Editor*
Donald J. Crump, *Associate Editor*
Philip B. Silcott, *Senior Editor*
Mary Ann Harrell, *Managing Editor*
Patricia F. Frakes, *Senior Researcher;*
 Bonnie S. Lawrence, Annmarie Manzi,
 Researchers

Illustrations and Design
William L. Allen, *Picture Editor*
Jody Bolt, *Art Director*
Suez B. Kehl, *Assistant Art Director*
Christine K. Eckstrom, Jane R. McCauley,
 Carolyn L. Michaels, Joan Straker,
 Edward O. Welles, Jr., *Picture Legends*
John D. Garst, Jr., Charles W. Berry, Margaret
 A. Deane, Alfred L. Zebarth, *Map Research,
 Design, and Production*

Production and Printing
Robert W. Messer, *Production Manager*
George V. White, *Assistant Production Manager*
Raja D. Murshed, June L. Graham,
 Christine A. Roberts, *Production Assistants*
Debra A. Antonini, David H. Battaglia,
 Cynthia E. Breeden, Jane H. Buxton,
 Mildred W. Forrest, Rosamund Garner,
 Suzanne J. Jacobson, Amy E. Metcalfe,
 Cleo Petroff, David V. Showers,
 Katheryn M. Slocum, Suzanne Venino,
 Staff Assistants
Kathryn Bazo, *Translations*
Barbara L. Klein, *Index*

Overleaf: Author George Stuart and colleague
Arthur G. Miller at a ruined temple at Tancah,
Quintana Roo. *Page 1:* Figurine, some 1,200
years old, from the burial island of Jaina. *Book-
binding:* Design blending traditional Maya and
Spanish Catholic symbols, from a huipil woven in
1977 at Larrainzar in highland Chiapas, Mexico.

*Shield Jaguar the Great holds the manikin
scepter that marks him as ruler of the
ancient Maya city of Yaxchilán. Before him
stands a lady probably his consort. Glyphs
above her yield a date equal to* A.D. *709.*

Foreword

Archeological field work in the Maya area tends to be more grueling than dangerous these days. Staggering from the hammock at four a.m., enduring 18-hour days of work and heat, preyed upon by innumerable delighted insects, and prompted to inward musings by internal rumblings, the archeologist often wonders whatever led him to choose this line of work. Gene and George Stuart are well aware of this, having put in their share of field time. Fortunately, however, they have kept their focus on the intellectual and esthetic rewards of Maya archeology.

Over time, these rewards have become more intricate, more human, and more interesting. Always there are the visual pleasures which surprise us whether we have spent 5 or 50 years in the field—I, for one, never fail to be moved by the dramatic temples of Tikal. But there are deeper matters. Only 20 years ago we thought of nameless groups of priest-rulers in their ceremonial centers, more starry-eyed and otherworldly than any group of intellectuals before or since. We now know that this picture was literally in-human. Reading their hieroglyphic texts, we can talk with some confidence of "Lord Pacal" of Palenque or "Stormy Sky" of Tikal. We also know that the Maya, once considered the most peaceful ancient people in Meso-america, were no better than we at avoiding war. Recent research has not only confirmed the defensive function of the great fortress of Becan, but has also detected defense works at other centers.

In addition, we now compare population densities in the lowland regions. We calculate the difference in stature between members of the ancient elite and commoners, finding that the elite were taller and therefore presumably better-fed. With such data we try to reconstruct the societies that developed civilized life. We have worked out elaborate systemic explanations for the origins of Maya civilization, and its collapse, and we test these against newly excavated information. We draw upon analogies from history, and note striking parallels between the end of the Middle Ages in Europe and the Maya collapse.

And yet, some things in Maya studies do not change very much. Patterns of everyday life still survive from the ancient past. The late Sir Eric Thompson depended heavily in some cases, and rightly so, on insights into ancient culture drawn from his study of the living Maya. In this book the Stuarts share their deep knowledge of traditional Maya communities. They show that the Maya have lost much of the extraordinary ancient achievement, and undergone 450 years of colonial and modern experience, but in their thatched houses and their cornfields represent at least the folk segment of their ancient civilization.

I have stood in the Petén rain forest and felt stunned by the magnitude of the task we have undertaken: to reconstruct and understand a civilization. Calculated conservatively, the past 100 years of archeological work has probably tapped less than 5 percent of the information that awaits us. While we have advanced greatly in our understanding, and employ elegant mathematical procedures that the ancient Maya would have appreciated, we are only approaching the most profound questions we must ask. Much of the old mystery remains. The Stuarts have blended all these elements admirably in the book which follows.

RICHARD E. W. ADAMS
The University of Texas at San Antonio

NATIONAL GEOGRAPHIC PHOTOGRAPHER OTIS IMBODEN

Contents

Working for a village association, a Maya potter of

Amatenango in highland Chiapas smooths a cooking vessel of traditional shape.

$\mathcal{S}$unrise contends
with mist in the
highlands of Guatemala
as a Maya fisherman plies
Lake Atitlán. A village
woman presses clothing
clean in the cold water.

Preceding pages:
Evening darkens the
volcanoes and steep
hillsides that rim the
lake, long a center of
highland culture. The
jagged terrain of this
area has always
hindered communication
among the Maya and
divided them into
clusters of settlements,
each with its own
distinctive customs.
Even today, some Maya
lakeside villages remain
accessible chiefly by boat.

Following pages:
In the lowland region
called the Petén,
temples rise above the
forest at Tikal. About
A.D. 800 this huge Maya
city may have covered
50 square miles and held
50,000 people. The
lowlands provided a
setting for the greatest
centers of Maya
civilization.

DAVID ALAN HARVEY
(OPPOSITE AND PRECEDING PAGES);
N.G.S. PHOTOGRAPHER OTIS IMBODEN
(FOLLOWING PAGES)

Old ways still
guide a highland farmer
from the village of
Chamula, in Mexico.
Stones plucked from
the earth mark
boundary lines. Like
his forefathers, he grows
corn and beans in
fields that lie fallow
between periodic
burnings. Long ago,
Maya farmers used
sophisticated techniques
such as terracing to
save soil. They had
plant strains improved
by centuries of selective
cultivation. By hand
labor, with tools of
stone and wood, they
succeeded in supporting
a large population—
and they provided the
indispensable basis of
an imposing civilization.

DAVID BRILL

ONE

Beginnings of the Maya Way

By George E. Stuart

Distinctive fabric and design of clothing mark this Maya woman and her children as residents of the highland farming community of Sololá, near Lake Atitlán. Patterns vary from village to village, a tradition that goes back at least to the Spanish Conquest.

A GREAT BLUE HERON led our motorboat upriver between banks of tangled green jungle. As we rounded each bend, the solitary bird would be floating on the brown mirror of water. With wingtips and feet stirring brief circles, he would take off as if in slow motion, glide ahead, then bank sharply around the next bend to await us once more. After a dozen turns in this game of grace, the heron suddenly wheeled up a narrow tributary, and the forest seemed to close forever behind him.

Photographer Otis Imboden and I had come to the Petén region of Guatemala to see an important new archeological discovery: several carved stone monuments found in the jungle near the Maya ruin called Dos Pilas. We were on the Petexbatún River, en route to the discovery site.

The Petén has held its secrets well. Among them are ruins of the sort that have made the ancient Maya famous as a vanished civilization. Crumbling pyramids, vine-shrouded walls, and fallen monuments fill much of this vast and desolate region—all that remains of a network of cities that flourished for many centuries before being abandoned about a thousand years ago. Dos Pilas had been such a city, and it had eluded discovery until 1960.

I wondered if the "new" monuments would be there when Otis and I arrived. Looters roam these parts in search of carvings and other salable artifacts for the illicit art market, and I had heard that one of the Dos Pilas stones had already been taken. Soon we would know if the others were still safe. Ian Graham, a research fellow of Harvard University's Peabody Museum of Archaeology and Ethnology, has made it his life work to record Maya monuments, and he was awaiting us at the site. A guide named Domingo, from nearby Sayaxché, would lead us overland to Ian's camp.

Our boat continued steadily up the meandering ribbon of the Petexbatún. The farmstead clearings scattered along the banks slowly gave way to a tropical landscape nearly untouched by modern man.

Brambles, gnarled trunks, and dark curtains of vine concealed the shadowy world away from the river. Cedars, mahoganies, sapodillas, and breadnuts towered above the tangle, their great branches punctuated by the dark starbursts of bromeliads.

Though the old cities lie deserted, ceiba trees still proclaim this a place of the Maya. According to their belief, this sacred tree of life dominated the center of the cosmos. On the Petexbatún, ceibas often grow precisely where meander curves afford the longest view. The bright path of water guided my eye time and time again to the tall slender bottle-shaped trunk of a ceiba, and to its symmetrical fan of foliage silhouetted against the clean, clear sky.

Then boatman Victor Manuel Ling cut the motor and turned to shore. Unseasonable rains had transformed our landing place to a plain of black mud. The steady breeze of the boat trip stilled, and the heat of the midmorning sun seemed determined to press us into the mire as we stepped ashore to sort our gear.

As the hum of Victor's boat receded downstream toward Sayaxché, Otis, Domingo, and I shared a hot Coca-Cola. Dos Pilas lay some ten miles inland—"Only a few hours' walk," Domingo assured us.

I recall the first mile or two well: sun-drenched clearings planted in interminable cornfields; the light shimmering off the stagnant pools in the great parallel ruts of a logging road; the hot weight of a cumbersome duffel bag on stony slopes. Otis devoted his energy to his heavy camera gear. We hardly spoke.

I remember wondering once where Domingo had gone, only to glimpse his burlap backpack down a narrow trail that had veered off into the dark shade of the forest—a welcome relief, except for the mud. Deeper than the trail was wide, it concealed the treacherous holes of hoofprints, for Ian Graham's packhorses had passed only a few days before. This path snaked up and down the slopes, around fallen trees, and across deceptively solid-looking clearings that threatened to suck off our boots.

Once a tiny cool stream crossed the trail. I pressed my face into it until mud touched my nose.

After three hours—and six rest stops—a long lunch break renewed our energy. We had come halfway, and the sun was lower. The forest grew cooler. More often now, or so it seemed, our crackling steps on twigs and fallen palm fronds gave way to silent plodding on firm ground. As dusk deepened the shadows beneath the immense tiers of vegetation, a new sound joined the cries and squawks of the birds out of sight above: the steady sound of chopping.

"Llegamos—we are arriving," Domingo remarked laconically.

Ian Graham, his khakis somewhat begrimed by his day in the field, welcomed us to the camp clearing. He had just returned from the newly discovered carvings, a half hour's walk away.

"You're in time. We can begin turning over the monuments tomorrow. Two of them are face down, so the carvings may be in good shape."

"Have any more been stolen?" I asked.

"Luckily, no. Government custodians for Dos Pilas have been guarding them since the looting. We only lost the one."

In the half light of evening, Ian gave Otis and me a brief tour of the main plaza of Dos Pilas. At very early Maya settlements, houses group themselves around a courtyard. At larger sites, this becomes a plaza, leveled and paved with limestone cement, flanked by platforms and shrines. At cities like Dos Pilas, temples rose beside the plaza, and the tall stone slabs called stelae recorded notable events. Now the plaza was a shadowy rectangle of grass surrounded by overgrown mounds. The fallen stelae lay here and there, protected from the rains by thatch shelters.

By nightfall we had hung our hammocks from the rafters of the thatch-roofed camp house, bathed at one of the deep springs, and eaten. At nine o'clock Ian cut off the tiny portable generator. The single light bulb slowly dimmed, leaving only the glow of the cook fire under its lean-to of palm. I dozed off listening to the hollow roar of a distant howler monkey.

Next morning, shafts of bright green light marked the end of the new trail to the discovery site. A wide stairway protruded from a slope; tree roots had displaced its great limestone blocks. It led us to a terrace. Beyond, and higher, lay another, and there I found all that was left of the stolen monument.

The looters had sawed through the thick base to detach the carved shaft. A clean job. The sawed surface was smooth, almost greasy to my touch. A large pile of bright stone chips the size of oyster shells lay nearby.

"They thinned the carved part of the stela here," Ian said grimly. "I've collected samples. At least we'll know the stone when and if it shows up on the market. The style should be recognizable, too, as that of the Dos Pilas sculptors."

Another stela lay face up and badly weathered. On the lower terrace Ian pointed out two more. One, barely visible, was anchored in the buttress roots of a giant breadnut tree. The other, a thick slab more than a yard wide and five yards long, lay face down. At some time long past it had fallen across a circular stone altar that protruded from the dark soil.

Ian and his helpers had tunneled under the stela to check for the presence of a carved inscription, then inserted pads of foam rubber to protect it. They had wedged short logs beneath the six-ton mass and built a huge log tripod over it, tying the rig together with thick ropes anchored by a sturdy tree.

"We have some text and some sharp relief—no question about that," Ian told me, "and it seems in good condition. Try it for yourself."

Cautiously, not to damage any fragile detail, I reached into the darkness under the stone. My palm lightly touched the

Intricate figures and hieroglyphs crowd the surface of a limestone stela, or carved monument, recovered in 1977 at Dos Pilas, a site in the Petén. The principal figure, in regalia that includes a mask headdress, represents a ruler of Dos Pilas now called Shield-God K. A water bird and a dwarf stand at his feet; a bound captive crouches below a glyph band. The carving records a date corresponding to December 3, A.D. 711.

familiar grid of deep grooves that separate the glyph blocks, or units, of a hieroglyphic inscription; then I felt an area of complicated detail. Here and there, my fingertips met the smooth areas of background.

All was ready. Mario, one of the government guards, stepped to the anchor tree where a hand winch interrupted the span of rope. He began to work its lever in careful rhythm. The ropes tightened slowly; the logs beneath the stone twitched and locked against the foam pads; the huge tripod sank to firmer footing and held. At last, the edge of the monument began its almost imperceptible lift—less than a quarter of an inch with each click of the lever.

Ian and I scurried back and forth, placing more brace logs in case something broke: "That end O.K.?" "Bring me a longer prop!" "Right!"

Finally the monument lay on one long edge stabilized by its own weight and, for the first time in many centuries, sunlight touched its carved face.

The principal figure of the relief stood larger than life. His face, turned in left profile, appeared half hidden by a scaly, round-eyed mask connected to a towering headdress of graceful feathers. He wore elaborate regalia, his sandaled feet resting on a band of symbols and star glyphs.

His left hand grasped a round shield, turned to display the handle strap. His right hand held the manikin scepter—the small image of a god with one leg ending in the form of a serpent—that identifies royal personages on many Maya sculptures. Flanking the dominant figure stood two others, much smaller: a turbaned dwarf wearing a jaguar-skin skirt, and a water bird holding a fish in its beak. At the base of the scene crouched a bound human figure, undoubtedly a captive.

"Dos Pilas style," Ian remarked to Otis, "a bit grandiose."

Above everything, between the incurving edges of the rounded top of the stela,

lay a panel of 18 glyph blocks—the main inscription. I studied it eagerly.

The first two columns held the Maya date. I consulted the special conversion tables I had optimistically brought along: The equivalent was December 3, A.D. 711. The only other element obvious at first inspection was the final glyph. This was the "emblem glyph," probably the place-name, of Tikal, the great site 70 miles northeast of Dos Pilas.

The most remarkable thing about the new find was this: Even as we labored to turn it that day at Dos Pilas, our Australian colleague Peter Mathews at Yale University had just predicted its existence.

Peter had been working with Ian's drawing of the long inscription on the back of Stela 8, another monument from Dos Pilas. He had isolated the name of a hitherto unknown ruler, "Shield-God K," so nicknamed for components of his name glyph. According to Stela 8, this ruler had lived from A.D. 673 to 726. Peter knew that during this lifetime, several important calendar cycles had passed. He also knew that the Maya would certainly have erected monuments to mark these. Field work ought to produce them.

Only a few weeks after the Dos Pilas trip, I ran into Peter at an archeology symposium in Guatemala City. We had barely greeted each other when he said, "I hear that you were there when the new monuments were turned."

"Yes, and I brought you copies of the photographs we made."

I pulled the prints from my briefcase and handed them to Peter. It took him only a second or two to find what he wanted.

"It's here—the right date and the name of the same bloke I've got! Thank goodness! I'm giving a paper on him tomorrow, and this clinches it."

Thus two instances of research confirmed the existence of an ancient American ruler. Perhaps eventually we'll be able to decipher the other glyphs on the new stela. If the looters didn't destroy the stolen one—

sometimes they saw up inscriptions to suit-case size—we may recover that text. At least we now had a date, a place, and an individual. And for me, the episode provided another precious glimpse into the special world of the Maya, whose land I have returned to time and time again over the past twenty years.

The Maya story is but part of a larger epic enacted between what is now north central Mexico and the western reaches of Honduras, Nicaragua, and Costa Rica. Anthropologists call this area Mesoamerica, and define its extent by the kind of culture shared by the peoples who lived there before the Spanish Conquest.

Maya territory covers roughly the eastern half of Mesoamerica, and coincides with the Yucatán Peninsula and its broad base. The Maya area is about half the size of Texas. It includes all of Guatemala and Belize, western Honduras and El Salvador, and most of Mexico east of the Isthmus of Tehuantepec—the states of Yucatán, Campeche, and Quintana Roo, most of Chiapas, and part of Tabasco.

Long before man came, nature divided the Maya area into distinct zones. *Highlands* extend from Chiapas across southern Guatemala into Honduras and El Salvador. Of the two *lowland* zones, one forms a narrow band along the Pacific; the other curves eastward along the Gulf Coast, then widens to form the great Peninsula of Yucatán.

Anthropologists usually refer to the half of Mesoamerica west of the Maya simply as "Mexico." Its many astonishing civilizations—from that of Teotihuacán to those of the Toltec, Mixtec, and Aztec—paced the Maya development, and often had a profound influence upon it.

Like the rest of Mesoamerica, the area of the Maya is washed by tropical rains that come, as a rule, between May and October. Varying amounts of rain, coupled with regional differences of elevation, soil, and terrain, have created a landscape of remarkable variety. Here, the Maya and their ancestors have lived for some 4,500 years.

* Cities and towns
▲ Archeological sites
◒ Populated places of archeological importance

In the heartland of Mesoamerica—regions of highly developed cultures and brilliant civilizations before the Spanish Conquest —Maya lifeways developed and flourished. The Maya area extends eastward from the Isthmus of Tehuantepec; west and north of it lies non-Maya country that archeologists call "Mexico"— shorthand for a portion of the modern nation. Comparatively ill-defined, the southern limits of the Maya area varied over the centuries.

oday, the Maya number approximately two million. They speak some 24 highland and lowland languages, related about as closely as the various Romance tongues. These languages have gradually changed over time, much as Chaucer's English evolved into that of Hemingway. Other ways, however, have changed remarkably little; and these underscore the fundamental continuity of tradition that has persisted in spite of the momentous culture changes and crises of the Mesoamerican past. Maya house types come immediately to mind.

Several years ago, my friend Esteban Cen supervised the construction of our family house at Cobá, a ruin and a living village in Quintana Roo state, Mexico. He and his crew spent weeks selecting, cutting, and dressing the proper logs and saplings for main supports, beams, and poles. These would form the walls of the long rectangle with rounded corners. The crew hauled in load after load of special thatch palm to be bound and bent around the poles of the steep roof frame. Finished in several weeks of part-time labor, the sturdy building—a work of art in itself—was a perfect kind of dwelling for the area. It survived a hurricane in good condition. Moreover, it duplicated other houses that appear in the region in murals a thousand years old.

Evidence of another house, virtually identical to ours at Cobá, is among the earliest traces of man in the Maya area. That house stood almost 4,500 years ago in what is now northern Belize. At the time, much of the Maya area was a vacant wilderness. Not, however, the Cuello site. Deep beneath the mounds that dot the surface there, Norman Hammond of Rutgers University has exposed part of the ancient platform and the dark stains of its postholes.

"The structure was very small," Norman told me at a recent archeological convention, "no more than 18 feet across, and round or oblong—we don't know which. We do know that it's the earliest example of architecture known in the Maya area."

Norman found something more at the bottom of his pit. The earliest pottery of Cuello lies there on bedrock, and radiocarbon readings from charred wood insist persuasively that it dates from about 2600 B.C.—earlier than any other sherds yet excavated in Mesoamerica.

By no means beginner's work, the Cuello pottery represents a remarkably sophisticated collection of plates, bowls, and graceful vases. It uses at least six surface colors: cream, orange, red, brown, black, and gray. Some pieces are decorated with geometric patterns of incised lines, others with small effigies of animals.

Where did the Cuello tradition begin, and when? "We don't know yet," says Norman briskly, "and if you want a wild opinion, ask somebody else!" Its role in the development of Maya culture remains to be sorted out. Its earliest pottery style has already been identified at Becan, near the center of the Yucatán Peninsula, and Maní, to the north. Its earliest date offers a convenient marker for the beginning of what archeologists call the Preclassic Period in Mesoamerica—and moves that beginning backward by about a thousand years.

If Cuello shows how little we really know about the ebb and flow of culture around 2500 B.C., other sites scattered over Mesoamerica give us a more complete picture of life a thousand years later. One of the best examples lies near Ocós, a fishing village on the Pacific Coast in Guatemala.

The landscape is uninspiring. The hot, nearly featureless plain holds dense thickets of brush and cactus dominated by fan palms. Despite the marginal rainfall, farmers here boast of an annual triple harvest of corn from the rich volcanic soil. The fishermen of Ocós draw upon the bounty of nearby lagoons and waterways.

The low mounds of La Victoria lie in a cattle pasture two miles north of the village. Between 1500 and 800 B.C., the land was quite different. A small settlement occupied

Faces and fashions from life in the Classic Period of Maya civilization appear in fired clay. Thousands of these figurines, probably portraits, have come from graves on the island of Jaina off the Gulf Coast of Yucatán. Many, fashioned with hollow bodies, served as ritual rattles or whistles. Blue paint has weathered less than the other colors that originally brightened the effigies. From left: A musician in a feathered headdress shakes a pair of rattles; a seated ballplayer wears the heavy padding used in Maya games; a priest holds a shield of Mexican style; a seated woman weaves cloth on a hand loom; a nobleman wears an elaborate headdress; a bearded man sits on a throne; a dignitary sports a wide-brimmed hat and a quilted coat; another ballplayer crouches for action.

a finger of land that jutted into mangrove-lined tidal estuaries. Analysis of La Victoria's remains allowed archeologist Michael D. Coe of Yale University to reconstruct life as it must have been during those days.

"A compact little community of ten or so houses with thatched roofs and gleaming white walls," Mike envisions. "Some of the men would be fishing and hunting turtles from their dugouts in the estuary, or hunting with dogs and nets in the forest, while others would be tending the corn in *milpa* clearings. A few women and children, knee-deep in estuary mud, would be feeling around for mollusks, and putting them into baskets while other women would be grinding soaked corn in the houses."

Surely an unspectacular picture, but one that epitomizes a self-sufficient life in the second millennium B.C.

Already some hints of a world to come appear at La Victoria: Small clay figurines of women, perhaps fertility fetishes, suggest simple religious cults. A wide range of pottery styles reflects ever-increasing networks of trade to provide for the needs of a growing population. Soon, the seeds of civilization would be added to those of corn, beans, and squash.

esoamerica took its first long stride toward civilized life on the hot, humid plain of the Veracruz Gulf Coast. This incredibly fertile land, with rich levees of silt along its sluggish rivers, had lured farmers to the area by 1500 B.C. No one knows what developments took place over the next few centuries, but they gave birth to a new kind of society.

The archeologists who first saw its sophisticated remains simply could not believe their extreme antiquity. Therefore, they named the culture after the people who lived in the Veracruz-Tabasco lowlands just before the Spanish Conquest. They were wrong, but the name "Olmec" stuck—confusingly enough.

The researches of the late Matthew W.

Stirling and his successors have clarified the story. These Olmec appeared on the Mesoamerican scene around 1200 B.C. and flourished for some eight centuries.

The Olmec have left testimonials to prodigious human labor. Their earliest site dates from the centuries between 1200 and 900 B.C. This, at San Lorenzo in Veracruz, is a man-made plateau containing 140 million cubic feet of fill. At La Venta, Tabasco, the Olmec center until 400 B.C., lies a mile-long set of platforms, replete with massive sculptures.

Olmec art is pervaded by the theme of the "were-jaguar," a form half man, half beast. Typically, a being with a smooth, almost infantile human body, a cleft or otherwise deformed head, and the drooping, snarling mouth of the feline. Carved scenes suggest that these eerie beings were associated with the sky, rain, and lightning.

"But that's not all," David Joralemon of Yale told me after completing a methodical analysis of Olmec motifs. "There were at least ten gods in the pantheon. Besides the were-jaguar, we now have the fire-serpent, a deity associated with the earth, and, naturally, a corn god."

Olmec sculptors, who created Mesoamerica's first great art style, carved the were-jaguar theme and others into exquisite if melancholy effigies of blue-green jade, or into monumental thrones that—along with the famed colossal heads—lined their ceremonial precincts.

Outside the Gulf Coast heartland, Olmec traces appear in pottery decoration, cave paintings, and boulder reliefs. They range from Mexico's central plateau to Guerrero, and from Oaxaca to El Salvador. Two important Olmec finds lie within the Maya lowlands: At Xoc, Chiapas, the imposing relief of a man with taloned feet and a snarling bird mask appears to stride across the face of a huge boulder—or did until recently, when the carving was cut off and stolen. And the glaring visage of a cleft-head being decorates a worn stela found just east of the Usumacinta River.

Some of these far-flung signs of the Olmec may indicate the presence of traders among the other rapidly developing peoples of Mesoamerica. Others suggest military expeditions or colonial outposts.

Almost as suddenly as they appeared, the Olmec vanished around 400 B.C. Many of their ways would endure to become part of the culture of later peoples—among them, the Classic Maya, who would appear seven centuries later in another area.

"One of the many Olmec-Maya links," Mike Coe explains, "is their mutual emphasis on the personality and power of political leaders. They both practiced a kind of warfare in which the humbling of captives counted a great deal. Besides that, we've got the ritual ball game common to both, along with specific bloodletting sacrifices, and the ritual use of mirrors. And look at the gods Joralemon is finding in Olmec art. Many of them are direct ancestors of those of the Maya."

The links are strengthened even more by the archeological remains from the centuries between 400 B.C. and A.D. 300, particularly those of Izapan culture.

Izapa, one of the greatest centers of the post-Olmec world, lies amid the green hills of the Pacific lowland of Chiapas, a scant 20 miles north of La Victoria. The place possessed certain important advantages. For one, the land and climate were perfect for cacao, a principal medium of exchange in pre-Hispanic Mesoamerica. In addition, Izapa was the gateway to the fertile band of lowland that stretched southeastward between the highlands and the sea.

Some 80 platforms of clay faced with river cobbles survive at Izapa, along with nearly 250 upright stone monuments—some with round "altars" in front. Fifty of the stelae are carved with cluttered narrative scenes of fantastic ritual and myth.

One depicts storm gods gathering water; another, bird gods in the sky; and still another, gods riding in canoes. In one macabre scene, a warrior brandishes a severed head—evidently the trophy of the

Messages from the past survive . . . or shatter: A Maya bowl from the Petén, considered one of the most significant ever found, implies a macabre world of rite and myth. Glyphs suggest an Underworld setting. Among the figures around it, a jaguar writhes upon a throne of bones. Others include a skeleton in jaguar garb, and a woman with a sacrificed infant. Below, only fragments remain of a funerary piece from Naachtún. Looters surprised at that site evidently dropped the bowl as they fled.

enemy whose body lies at the victor's feet.

The style and motifs of these Izapa carvings fit well between those of the Olmec and the art of the Classic Maya. Indeed, the continuity of several specific motifs is readily apparent to art historians like Jacinto Quirarte of the University of Texas at San Antonio.

"There's the U-shaped element that Mike Coe reads as 'moon,'" Jacinto told me; "I read it as a reference to the jaguar or feline—anyway, it carries right on through. So do the crossed bands or 'Saint Andrew's cross.' And the long-lipped god is clearly a precursor of the Maya rain god."

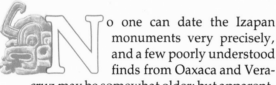o one can date the Izapan monuments very precisely, and a few poorly understood finds from Oaxaca and Veracruz may be somewhat older; but apparently Izapan art is the first to include two crucial elements of the Classic Maya world—the calendar and hieroglyphic writing.

Not long ago, Gareth Lowe of the New World Archaeological Foundation showed me a thin fragment of polished limestone from an Izapan site. Engraved on it were bars and dots—number symbols, in the sequence that ancient Mesoamericans employed to record dates in their complex calendar. Though incomplete, this date can be equated to December 5, 36 B.C. If the reading is correct, the little slab I so carefully held bears the earliest recorded date in the New World. The Classic Maya, using the very same system, would not carve *their* earliest known date until A.D. 292.

Southeast of Izapa, the Pacific Slope of Guatemala holds remains of virtually every age of Mesoamerican prehistory, but only a handful of its hundreds of sites have ever been excavated. Indeed, the very richness of the place has often served only to confuse the record.

For two seasons, John Graham and Robert Heizer, both of the University of California at Berkeley, have supervised excavations and mapping at Abaj Takalik, a huge site that sprawls across four different coffee plantations in the fertile piedmont.

Not long ago, Gene, John, and I stood near one of the many mounds in the coffee grove beside the stony old road that traverses the site. A large pit, carefully placed to avoid damage to the delicate coffee trees, reached two yards down into the reddish volcanic soil.

"The white layer near the surface," John was saying as he pointed to the smooth face of the excavation wall, "is the 1902 ash fall that covered everything here. Below that, we have everything else. The stela there—the stumpy one we've listed as Stela 5—has a date that works out to A.D. 126, but that's not the most interesting thing about it. Look at the style of the figure. I think it's definitely more Maya than Izapan. In fact, to me, it looks very much like a very early Maya carving."

John pointed to another pit nearby.

"There we found part of an Olmec colossal head, de-faced and re-carved into some sort of figure seated in a niche; up in the garden of the plantation house is one of those exasperating potbellied figures that no one has figured out yet.

"And our biggest problem is that whoever lived here in the Late Classic decided to *reset* all the Preclassic monuments. So far, it seems as if we've excavated the New World's first museum."

As we started the dusty ride back, Gene spotted something in a gully: *"Look!* What's that? A carved stone?" I stopped the van abruptly and John hopped out to investigate.

"Just one of the old kilometer markers. We have to check everything here, though. A rounded stone right in this road turned out to be one of our best monuments."

Whatever its complications, Abaj Takalik brings the post-Olmec world closer in time and style to the Maya lowlands of the far north. Between the two places lie the highlands—and Kaminaljuyú.

It's not much to look at, that series of grassy humps in a Guatemala City suburb. Bits of litter scud here and there in the cool breeze of the lofty plateau, and a low chain-link fence wards off halfheartedly the encroaching rows of new housing. But beneath the surface, the many layers of Kaminaljuyú's antiquity hold, among other things, the crowning glory of the world that gave birth to Maya civilization.

Accidentally breached by the expansion of a soccer field in 1935, the mounds of Kaminaljuyú were not long in revealing their part in the story of the centuries between 100 B.C. and A.D. 200.

Tombs of what archeologists term the Miraflores phase were among the most dazzling ever found in Mesoamerica. The honored dead, wrapped in finery, were buried on wooden litters with sacrificed retainers nearby. In one of the richest tombs, more than 300 objects of the finest workmanship—stone bowls and bottles, plaques of jade mosaic, pottery vessels of outrageous variety—nearly covered the floor.

Shaded by a parasol, Anne Cary Maudslay visits broken stelae carved by Maya artists at Quiriguá, in lowland Guatemala. She accompanied her husband, the English explorer and archeologist Alfred Percival Maudslay, on a visit to the area in 1894. He had spent months surveying the site and making molds and photographs of sculpture —the first serious scientific study of this important center. The meticulous accuracy of his work here and elsewhere eased the task of deciphering Maya inscriptions.

Investigating the origins of the Maya, John A. Graham examines a stone altar at Abaj Takalik, near the Pacific Coast of Guatemala. Behind it, Stela 5 bears a date equal to A.D. 126—possibly early Maya work. Below, he opens a stone box of unknown date and obscure style, found nearby in February 1977. Its contents, from Late Classic times, include a jade pendant, beads, and miniature pottery vessels. The site has also yielded major monuments of the Olmec culture, first high culture of Mesoamerica. As the first site with Olmec and Maya monuments side by side, Abaj Takalik may clarify the rise of Maya civilization.

For me, the whole accomplishment of the cosmopolitan and literate people of the Miraflores phase is embodied in the bas-relief black stone known prosaically as Stela 10. Only fragments of this immense monument survive. These show parts of three figures in rich and assured detail. One brandishes a scepter or weapon of chipped flint. Another, bearded and fanged, bends forward. Large ornate glyphs—perhaps calendrical names—accompany the beings. Beside one is a long text decisively engraved in small glyphs. These appear at first glance to be Classic Maya, but in fact are not—and at present they cannot be read.

The Preclassic roots of the Maya, like those of the ceiba trees that line their rivers, are woven into an almost inextricable tangle. The many roots of the ceiba, however, are traceable if one takes the trouble to do so. Those of the Classic Maya are not, for many peoples made their contributions over a very long time. The time elapsed between the beginning of Olmec culture and that of the Classic Maya world roughly equals the interval that separates us from the fall of Rome.

Thus the beginnings of Maya civilization are obscure, but in a familiar human way. Before 2500 B.C. and afterward, Mesoamericans were never proceeding along isolated lines of development.

Rather, as closely related peoples have always done, they were constantly exchanging, selecting, and modifying ideas to suit their particular needs. And, as the water bird on our stela at Dos Pilas reminds us, they found inspiration in their natural world.

Late one afternoon, I stood alone on the worn summit of one of the highest mounds left at Kaminaljuyú listening to the yells of a pickup soccer game in the ancient plaza below, and to the noise of rush-hour traffic on the Calzada San Juan. I looked north, toward a cloud bank that lay high in the direction of the Petexbatún River, and wondered what the great blue heron was doing.

Deep in the Petén, at Dos Pilas, a team wrests Maya sculptures from the earth—its leader, Ian Graham of Harvard's Peabody Museum. At right, workers hack a stela free from the grip of a breadnut tree whose roots had grown across it; a preliminary check has shown that the hidden side bears carving. The author takes time out to sip water warm from the canteen. Then a rig of ropes, poles, and hand winch lifts the stela to its side while Graham checks a padded bracing pole. The Scottish explorer-scholar has dedicated himself to drawing and photographing all known Maya inscriptions.

Mutilated fragments of stone lie scattered at La Naya, a site in the Petén. Looters often chisel or saw away the carvings of stelae to sell in the art market. In 1971 one of Ian Graham's men was killed by gunshots when his group surprised looters at work here.

S cene of ancient sport inspires impromptu soccer as schoolboys play on the Maya ball court at Iximché, Guatemala. From the sixth century B.C., varying versions of a ball game spread across Mesoamerica, each region apparently developing special rules and costumes. Below, echoes of past contests haunt a court at Copán. Here, near the famous Hieroglyphic Stairway, players competed i a strenuous game that combined sport and ceremony. Knowledge of the events comes from surviving courts, sculpture, and ceramics. The vase at left shows players in front of "end zone" steps. Overleaf: A re-creation captures the tension of the contest.

TWO

An Age of Splendor

By George E. Stuart

Hallmark of the Maya golden age: Richly carved headdress frames the serene face of a noblewoman on a stela at Copán. Between A.D. *250 and 900, while their civilization flourished, the Maya erected such monuments to commemorate significant occasions in the lives of rulers and of dynasties.*

TIME. Maya priests of the Classic Period likened it to an endless procession of gods who were really numbers. These beings walked their eternal trail bent low by the heavy loads that pulled their tumplines hard against their perspiring foreheads. The burdens—great animals and birds—were gods too, the patrons of individual days or certain multiples of days. This awesome procession moved through the Maya eternity in careful mathematical order.

The *lub*, or resting place, for the number gods corresponded to whatever day was current. At any given time, the priests knew, five number gods would be seated beside their cargoes on the sacred woven mat. By their very presence and combination, they and their burdens would reflect the exact number of days that had elapsed since the beginning of the calendar count.

The resting place for the day we would recognize as July 24, A.D. 736, was memorialized by the sculptors of Stela D at Copán, Honduras, one of the most imposing of the Classic Maya cities.

Late one November afternoon not long ago, I stood at the north end of Copán's main plaza, behind the ornate monument. There, the relentless procession of time was frozen in the dark stone.

Number Nine, a handsome youth with the spots of the celestial serpent on his chin, sits leaning forward, his jade necklace dangling against one knee. His right hand reaches to adjust his tumpline. It holds the giant screech owl of the *baktun*, the 144,000-day period. Together the two represent nine times 144,000, or 1,296,000 days.

In the next hieroglyphic block reclines a nearly toothless, wrinkled old man with the *tun*, possibly a drum, as his headdress. His face and headgear mark him as the number Five, but closer inspection shows that he has the fleshless lower jaw of Ten, the death god. The combination represents Fifteen. He embraces the large bird that is regent of the *katun*, the period of 7,200 days. Fifteen times 7,200 equals 108,000.

The next number god on Stela D is

definitely Five, for the old man has a normal jaw. He straightens his headdress, but with difficulty, since he appears to be distracted by the huge winged being, half serpent, half bird—the *tun*, or 360-day period—that lies heavy and docile across Five's lap and left arm. Five times 360 is 1,800.

The number gods of the next two glyphs are young males whose lower jaws are formed by hands. Both represent Zero. One is arm-in-arm with a huge crouching toad, musician of the rain gods, who represents the 20-day *uinal*. The other holds the grotesque elongated arm of a human with a monkey face, one of the disguises of the sun god, patron of the *kin*, or single day. Their totals amount to nothing, for zero times anything—even a large toad—is zero.

All together, the five number gods and their companions on Stela D represent a total of 1,405,800 days—the interval between the beginning of the Maya day count and that summer day nearly 1,250 years ago.

Maya archeologists call a date of this kind a Long Count date or, since it usually introduces a longer text, an Initial Series date. There were, of course, much simpler methods of recording this five-place notation. Sometimes only the heads of the gods

were depicted. Most often, combinations of bars and dots—fives and ones, respectively—and special signs for zero sufficed, along with simple geometric forms to identify the time units.

Long Count reckonings reach back to a specific day. Most Mayanists agree that it is equal to August 10, 3114 B.C. Others insist that any correlation between the Gregorian and the Maya calendars is provisional at best. In any case, that noteworthy day was surely a milestone of myth, not history, for it falls well before the beginning of the Preclassic Period.

The Maya did not invent the Long Count. The columns of bars and dots that Gene and I saw on Gareth Lowe's limestone fragment and the monuments of Abaj Takalik are only a few of the Preclassic examples found between Veracruz and the Pacific Slope of Guatemala.

It remained for the Maya, who appear to have been obsessed with time and awed by the grandeur of its passage, to carry the Long Count to its most elaborate form. Their use of it in the lowlands of the Yucatán Peninsula serves to define the span of the Classic Period: A.D. 250 to 900, approximately. During those six and a half centuries, the Maya created one of the most distinguished civilizations of all antiquity.

"This was no priest-plus-peasant soci-

ety," declares William R. Coe of the University of Pennsylvania, "but a vastly stratified, cosmopolitan culture." Bill's comment is apt, for Classic Maya society was indeed complicated.

The elite controlled matters of government, warfare, religion, and commerce. Architects within this highest group designed great temples, palaces, and public buildings in a variety of brilliant regional styles. Skilled masons, members of a class that included servants of royalty and potters, erected the great stone buildings around the spacious plazas that characterize the Maya civic-ceremonial centers.

Priests of the Classic Period directed human participation in a supernatural realm governed by a bewildering hierarchy of gods who demanded continual homage and frequent penance. Painters and sculptors perpetuated the themes of religion and the cosmos, interlocked with the records of powerful rulers and the fortunes of their dynasties.

Maya astronomers never ceased their effort to refine the harmony of the moving universe with the ever-recurring cycles of time they had inherited from their Mesoamerican forebears. Scribes, meanwhile, dutifully recorded the texts of history and divination in the most complex writing system ever developed in the New World.

Scenes on this array of polychrome vases provide insight into Classic Maya life and belief. Three display a band with glyphs from a formula called the Primary Standard Sequence: possibly a prayer for the dead. Such superb ceramics usually come from the tombs of the elite, and suggest their pride. From left: A warrior, bedecked in a feathered back piece, carries a spear and a human head. Trumpet players entertain a ruler. In an Underworld setting, a dwarf offers birds to an aged lord seated on his throne. Flames engulf a man balanced on his back, in a depiction of the dance after a decapitation ceremony. Clasping a fan, a man stands before a throne on a unique vessel coated with fragile white stucco and painted with the famous "Maya blue." A ball-game player wears an elaborate bird headdress and jaguar-skin thigh pads. A fox god crouches in submission before a ruler of the Underworld.

VASES, FROM LEFT, ONE THROUGH SIX, FROM PRIVATE COLLECTIONS.
PHOTOGRAPHS BY NICHOLAS M. HELLMUTH, FOUNDATION FOR LATIN AMERICAN
ANTHROPOLOGICAL RESEARCH. SEVEN, FROM DUMBARTON OAKS COLLECTION,
WASHINGTON, D. C. PHOTOGRAPH BY OTIS IMBODEN.
ACTUAL HEIGHTS VARY FROM 6 TO 10 INCHES.

No less an achievement was that of the Maya farmer. Working in an indifferent, almost hostile, land where rainfall and yield were ever in delicate balance with poorish soil, the encroaching forest, and a nagging threat of drought, the Maya farmer won most of his battles. He slashed fields from the high forest, and constructed artificial plots—"raised fields"—in the swampy depressions of the unpromising *bajos*. These he irrigated with the help of canals or simply with vessels of water carried into the fields. Where he could, he erected terraces to capture precious rainfall. He not only grew corn, beans, and squash, but cultivated groves of fruit trees as well. He planted *ramón*, or breadnut trees, a source of food if the corn crops failed. Without his skills the great pyramid temples might never have risen above the jungle.

Like other archeologists, I have always been skeptical of the term "lost" for cities or civilizations. In general, even the most remote ruins are well known to the people living nearby. Not so with many of the Classic Maya cities, for in the end they were reclaimed by the very jungle that had sheltered them.

Classic Maya civilization was truly lost until the beginning of the 19th century, when brief notices of crumbling jungle cities began to appear in obscure publications. Thus was born the aura of mystery that ever seems to attend things Maya.

In 1822, Henry Berthoud of London published the *Description of the Ruins of an Ancient City, Discovered Near Palenque....* This thin squarish volume contained the account of one Antonio del Rio, an artillery captain who had been sent in 1786 by the Spanish Crown to search the ruins for treasure. Del Rio and 79 Maya Indians had attacked Palenque with crowbars and pickaxes.

"Ultimately," recalled the captain, "there remained neither a window nor a doorway blocked up, a partition that was not thrown down, nor a room, corridor, court, tower, nor subterranean passage in which excavations were not effected from two to three yards in depth, for such was the object of my mission."

Fortunately for us, del Rio did not find the gold he sought, but he and the explorers who came afterward discovered treasure of another sort—tangible evidence of an amazingly rich Maya past.

The ruins were more kindly treated—and best chronicled—by John Lloyd Stephens and artist Frederick Catherwood, who made two epic journeys through the Maya area between 1839 and 1842. Four volumes of engaging narrative and superb engravings resulted from the pioneer work of the pair. Every few years I reread Stephens's books, and I learn something new each time.

Even so, it is difficult to imagine the impact that the Maya ruins had upon those who saw them for the very first time. I came closest to that realization at the small ruin of Chicanná, near the geographical center of the Yucatán Peninsula. Jack D. Eaton, now of the University of Texas at San Antonio, had discovered the site in 1966. Before he excavated the ruins, he guided me there.

I first saw the building through the forest about a hundred feet away. Its three doorways opened upon sunlight, for the rooms behind had caved in. But not the front. The stone-and-stucco facade of the long structure imitated a gigantic monster face. Great eyes stared from above the central entrance, and huge stone teeth hung over the doorway—the mouth of the face. A rubble-covered (Continued on page 49)

Epic riddle in stone carvings, the Great Hieroglyphic Stairway rises behind a faceless stela at Copán. With more than 2,000 glyphs, the steps contain the longest of Maya texts. Long ago an earthquake dislodged and jumbled them; at present, as restored, they defy efforts to decipher them.

DAVID ALAN HARVEY

Tales of a mighty dynasty survive in stone sculptures at Quiriguá, where the tallest stelae and largest boulder monuments in the Maya world commemorate the eighth-century rule of the Sky family. Apparently, Cauac Sky, a lord from nearby Copán, led Quiriguá to assert political independence—and to flourish. Sky Xul assumed power after Cauac Sky and immortalized himself with the massive carved stone at right; archeologist David Sedat measures panels of hieroglyphs that record the succession of rulers. Below, Maya workers clear rubble from Quiriguá's acropolis area, scene of the 1975 discovery of a sun-god mask on a free-standing wall. Christopher Jones examines the stone-mosaic mask—erected during the reign of Cauac Sky.

In the footsteps of their forefathers, modern farmers practice slash-and-burn cultivation—one of many agricultural techniques used by the ancient Maya. On a dry spring day near Maní, Yucatán, Mario Antonio Raigosa cuts brush in his field as the fire he set clears the land for planting. His milpa, or cornfield, may smolder for several days. After the first rains, he will plant corn like the farmer at right, punching holes for the kernels with a dibble stick. During the Classic Period, the Maya relied on intensive agricultural methods to meet the demands of a growing population. With raised fields built up in swampy areas, and reservoirs for water storage, the Maya could support the densely inhabited centers of their civilization.

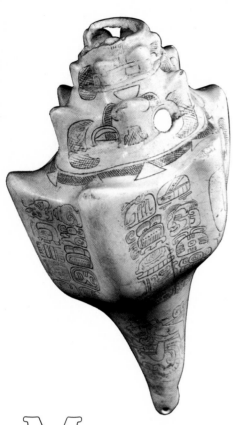

Masterworks from the hands of ancient artists reflect the rich tradition of painting and calligraphy in the Maya Classic age. Delicately incised glyphs decorate a rare conch-shell trumpet, once played for ritual events or to entertain a ruler. On a bichrome funerary vase—shown as a subtle composition by this rollout photograph—bold hieroglyphs and figures probably concern the fate of the dead in the Underworld. A dancer wields a tasseled ax as a costumed dwarf stands before an old lord; the black bird beneath his throne may represent the artist's signature.

VASE (ABOVE) FROM A PRIVATE COLLECTION; ROLLOUT PHOTOGRAPH © JUSTIN KERR, 1977

porch with a few teeth poking up through the dark leaf mold formed its lower jaw.

It was not the intricacy or the ornateness of the incredible structure, as I recall, that touched my emotions so. Rather, it was the contrast of the man-made symmetry with the wild and random tangle of vegetation that had all but reclaimed it. Chicanná will always be with me.

From the beginning, Maya ruins fostered speculations, many of them outlandish, on their proper place in world history. Jean Frédéric Maximilien, self-styled Comte de Waldeck, who had prepared del Rio's illustrations, came to see Palenque for himself in 1832. He believed that the ruins reflected the blend of all the great Old World civilizations of antiquity.

Half a century later, a self-taught savant named Augustus Le Plongeon took the opposite view. Bearded and dignified in appearance, unrestrained in speculation, and hotly cantankerous in argument, he identified the Maya area as the Garden of Eden. Zigzag motifs in a sculpted lintel convinced him that the Maya had invented the electric telegraph. In Yucatán, he insisted, all the world's civilizations were born.

Lately, the Maya are among those whose origins have been attributed to beings from outer space. This belief stems partly from the curious notion that people of the remote past were simply incapable of moving large stones or having a complex society, religion, or art. This is most unfair to the Maya and others who really do not need the convenient catchall of outer space to explain their accomplishments.

With the gestures of an orator and the garb of a nobleman, this Jaina figurine may in fact portray a dignitary delivering a speech. Feathered cape and tasseled loincloth apron suggest his lordly rank while his prominent nose represents the Classic Maya ideal of beauty.

Evidence accumulated over the past 150 years shows that the Maya epic is, in itself, a fascinating story of human achievement, and that it unfolded along familiar lines of cultural development and change. There are still many mysteries, even in the well-studied Petén. Otherwise archeology, Maya or not, wouldn't be any fun.

The Petén, hearth of the lowland Maya, stretches from the valley of the Usumacinta River eastward into Belize, and from the green foothills of the Guatemalan highlands northward into Mexico. From the air it appears as a vast trackless wilderness of jungle, broken here and there by grassy plains; but it is much more varied than it appears. Beneath the forest canopy, rough ridges of rotten limestone wrinkle the surface and shape the courses of the many rivers that feed the Usumacinta, the Pasión, and the Río Hondo. North of Lake Petén Itzá lies a land of fewer streams, but there the jungle hides expansive bajos, those great seasonal swamps that helped the ancient inhabitants of the land solve their eternal problem of water.

Mayanists agree that the Petén was uninhabited until around the beginning of the first millennium B.C., when farmers settled the banks of the Pasión River near the present town of Sayaxché.

"The earliest signs of people we found at Seibal," says Gordon R. Willey of Harvard University, the eminent Maya scholar who supervised excavation of the site, "were ceramics dating to just after 1000 B.C. These suggest connections with the highlands of Guatemala and El Salvador. There's a possible Gulf Coast link, too. We found a cache of the same date—polished jade axes arranged in the form of a cross. With them was one of those jade 'ice picks.' The whole thing had a very Olmec feel about it. Perhaps people were coming into the Petén from the northwest as well."

Numerous excavations over the entire Yucatán Peninsula have helped us reconstruct what may have happened thereafter. By 300 B.C. an expanding population had nearly filled the lowlands. By 50 B.C. the population had grown to a point where differences in land potential began coming into play. This must have fostered increasing competition over land and water.

"Political organization must have changed rapidly," says Richard E. W. Adams of the University of Texas at San Antonio. "The elite must have established themselves as rulers by hereditary right—a change from a career group to a caste, so to speak. And the ceremonial centers were expanding. Remember, these people were pacing their development through contact with sophisticated places like Chiapa de Corzo—where Gareth Lowe found that date fragment—and Kaminaljuyú."

A key chapter in the story of early Maya development surely lies beneath the great mounds of El Mirador that dominate the otherwise featureless horizon of the far northern Petén. Only a few people have visited El Mirador, among them Ian Graham. His preliminary survey shows more than 200 mounds and the remains of a dozen great pyramids. The site may be the largest in the entire Maya area—and the earliest as well, for the only known carvings there are two eroded fragments done in the late Preclassic style of Kaminaljuyú.

atural catastrophe may, too, have played a role in the development of Maya civilization. Sometime between A.D. 100 and 300, the volcano Ilopango blew up in central El Salvador. Payson Sheets of the University of Colorado has devoted years to the study of the eruption.

"We've seen the ash fall," Payson told me. "It covers much of central and western El Salvador, and its effects probably reached much farther. Near Ilopango, plants and animals directly in the path of the ash flows would have been killed instantly by heat and suffocation; survivors would face the immediate problems of shock, injury, and choking dust, soon followed by those of fouled water and a disrupted food supply. Things simply stopped, and as many as 30,000 people may have left the area. Probably many of these survivors moved north, into the Maya lowlands."

Payson's colleague Robert Sharer of the University of Pennsylvania directed the excavations at Chalchuapa, where the ash layer was first identified.

"Before the disaster," Bob told me just recently, "trade routes between Mexico and Central America followed the Pacific Coast. Afterward, the main routes crossed the Maya lowlands to the north. Possibly El Mirador was a significant trade center then. But you start getting tremendous implications when you think about Tikal. We know Tikal was inhabited by 600 B.C., and growing. It grows faster around the beginning of the Christian era. It really takes off a couple of centuries later—as if it had cornered this new trade pattern. And that's the beginning of Classic Maya civilization as we know it now."

Around the time of the birth of Christ there rose a city whose destiny and fortunes would profoundly affect those of the early Classic Maya world.

Teotihuacán, some 600 miles west of the central Petén, lies on Mexico's Central Plateau. By A.D. 200 the "Abode of the Gods" was a carefully planned and populous city of merchants, warriors, and ambitious rulers. Together they made Teotihuacán the most powerful political and cultural force of its time in Mesoamerica.

In the Maya area, archeologists first note the signs of Teotihuacán among the remains of Guatemala's Pacific Slope and at Kaminaljuyú, in the highlands. There the late Preclassic cultures still possess the Long Count, hieroglyphic writing, and other traits that obviously anticipate the later world of the Classic Maya of the lowlands. But suddenly, in a time of change, these highlanders seem to stop in their tracks and turn into Mexicans.

We don't know the nature of the takeover. I and others see it as a kind of "cordial

Lowland and highland terrain have
set their distinctive stamps on Maya
life from the beginning, with
Mexican influence especially strong
in the ancient highland communities.
Copán and Palenque mark approximate
limits of the Maya lowlands, which
extend through the Petén and the
Yucatán Peninsula. Here Classic
Maya civilization reached its
dazzling zenith of accomplishment.

Gulf of Mexico

Progreso
Dzibilchaltún
Mérida (Tihó)   Izamal Sitilpech
                              Valladolid
        YUCATÁN   (Saki)
Telchaquillo   Chemax
  Mayapán   Sotuta Chichén Itzá   Cobá
  Muna
Uxmal Maní Chumayel
Kabah   Oxkutzcab   Tulum Cozumel
  Sayil Labná   Island
      Yaxhachén
Jaina   QUINTANA
                           ROO
Campeche

                Felipe Carillo Puerto
                (Chan Santa Cruz)

Champotón

Bay of Campeche   YUCATÁN PENINSULA

              CAMPECHE

                    Becan   Chetumal
              Chicanná
                               Hondo
TABASCO   Usumacinta
Villahermosa   Calakmul

                              Altun Ha
          Palenque   El Mirador   Belize City

          Piedras Negras   Uaxactún   Barton Ramie
ERACRUZ   PETÉN Tikal Naranjo Belmopan
Chamula Nabenchauk   Lake Petén Itzá   BELIZE
Tuxtla Gutiérrez Tenejapa Yaxchilán Flores La Naya
Chiapa de Corzo San Cristóbal Bonampak (Tayasal)
AXACA Zinacantán de Las Casas Sayaxché
           Amatenango   Seibal
                                    Gulf of Honduras
CHIAPAS   Grijalva

                          Lake
                          Izabal
        GUATEMALA
                                Quiriguá
          Nebaj
        Huehuetenango   Motagua
      Utatlán Chichicastenango   Copán
Quezaltenango Sololá Míxco Viejo
Lake Atitlán   Iximché   HONDURAS
Abaj Takalik Kaminaljuyú Guatemala City

                          Pacific Ocean

              Chalchuapa Tazumal
          San Salvador Ilopango Volcano
                          EL SALVADOR

• Cities and towns
▲ Archeological sites
⌂ Populated places of archeological importance

0   100
KILOMETERS

0   100
STATUTE MILES

Pacific Ocean

NICARAGUA

conquest"—an overwhelming combination of military and commercial expansion by the empire builders of the distant city. Its effects for the Maya area were far-reaching and, for the highlands, indelible. From this time on throughout the prehistoric period, the southern Maya area would retain, in its ceramics and its architecture, a flavor as much Mexican as Maya.

"Gray morning in the Great Plaza at Tikal," begins one of the entries in my diary. "To my right and left, the steep stairs of Temples I and II reach literally into the clouds, for fog came in the night. All I am able to see of the summit buildings are their dark doorways and a hint of their towering roof combs. Ahead, the damp grass stretches to the row of dark monuments that fronts the wide stone stairway of the North Acropolis. The bulky silhouettes beyond are those of buildings constructed more than ten centuries ago—and those were merely the last raised on the North Acropolis. Under them lie the rubble-filled rooms, plaster floors, tombs, and debris of another thousand and a half years. There are many ghosts here—this morning, all of them seem to be wandering about."

Tikal, apparently the largest of the Classic Period Maya cities in the Petén, is truly a place of superlatives. It centers some 50 square miles of low house mounds. Roughly 3,000 major structures lie within the heart of Tikal, and these conceal an estimated 10,000 earlier constructions. Temple IV, with a roof comb thrust 212 feet into the Petén sky, is the tallest known building of antiquity east of Teotihuacán. And Stela 29, dated July 6, A.D. 292, has the earliest Long Count date known so far in the Maya lowlands.

For 14 years beginning in 1956, archeologists of the University of Pennsylvania, in cooperation with the government of Guatemala, subjected Tikal to the most intensive program of excavation in the history of Maya studies. Given Tikal, it seems they barely scratched the surface, but the 500 buildings excavated, the tons of artifacts analyzed, and the vast amounts of other data provide a remarkably detailed look into the lives and times of the Classic Maya world.

Clemency Coggins of Harvard has sifted and correlated much of this information into a tantalizing picture of personalities and power politics.

"My job was to analyze painting and drawing styles," she says. That meant dating the decorated ceramics from tombs of the elite, with evidence from dated monuments and architecture. Thus she built up a chronology and dynastic relationships. However tentative many of her conclusions may be, they fit the data beautifully.

Stormy Sky, like other Maya rulers, bears a modern nickname derived from his name glyph—a sky symbol surmounted by a long-nosed god with arms extended and a curious smoking object in his forehead.

His immediate predecessor, Curl Snout, was represented by an animal with a tight curl over the snout, above a mouth with prominent fangs. And Tikal's first identifiable ruler, Jaguar Paw of the early third century, had a distinctive glyph repeated in many later inscriptions.

Curl Snout ruled for 47 years, and grave goods from those decades show the style of Teotihuacán. Perhaps he had come from Kaminaljuyú as a trade emissary of high rank and married a daughter of the royal Jaguar Paw line.

Doubtless of royal birth, Stormy Sky himself came to power January 30, A.D. 426. One *katun* later, October 17, 445, the superb Stela 31 was dedicated to this important anniversary. Stormy Sky appears on the front of the stone, his name emblazoned in his headdress, an ancestral deity overhead. On his belt he wears the heads of the Maya sun god, Kinich Ahau, and the Jaguar God of the Underworld. Flanking him—smaller, but neither belligerent nor submissive —are two magnificent warriors dressed and armed in the style of Kaminaljuyú and

Teotihuacán. Thus a great king might honor a blended inheritance or a proud alliance.

. Stormy Sky died—possibly in battle—at the end of a distinguished reign. Tikal Project archeologists found his "Painted Tomb" in 1960. Its stuccoed interior bore a giant Long Count notation for March 18, A.D. 457—date of death? Of burial?—and numerous symbols that Clemency Coggins speculates may have been the cues for funeral chanters.

The body of the king, headless and handless, was flanked by those of two youths, recalling the figures on the commemorative stela. The tomb lies in line with that of his predecessor—an arrangement common at Kaminaljuyú.

The Early Classic world of Stormy Sky and his successors was one of rapidly developing civic-ceremonial centers scattered through the lowlands. Only a day's walk north of Tikal lay Uaxactún; four days farther, Calakmul; and past that, Becan.

The trails led everywhere, it must have seemed—through forests and cleared fields, across the bajos on raised roadways, and, where possible, along rivers.

While the number gods carried their burdens of time, mortals took the trails of earth—merchants, guides, and porters with shoulders bent under the load and tumplines taut against the forehead. The trade routes were long, as shown by a distinctive greenish-gold obsidian from the Teotihuacán area. David Pendergast of the Royal Ontario Museum found examples of it more than 700 miles away, in a second-century cache at Altun Ha, in Belize.

But there was danger on the trails as well. Becan's compact center was surrounded by a great dry moat some 50 feet wide, 17 feet deep, and more than a mile long. Clay and rock from the ditch formed a high parapet on the inner side. David Webster, who excavated part of the ditch, sums it up as a formidable defensive work. He dates it to the very beginning of the Classic Period, which means it was contemporary with the lovely Teotihuacán cache vessel

Unique in the Maya area, this crumbling life-size image came to light in 1967, in a remote cave in the Petén; rumor says that vandals have since destroyed it. It may have honored a rain god or a deity of the interior of the earth. Maya priests of ancient and more recent times collected dripwater from such caverns for ritual use, revering this "virgin" water as most sacred and pure.

IAN GRAHAM

and figurines found in Becan itself. Items of greenish-gold obsidian strengthen these associations, and Webster suggests that a further search for obsidian artifacts might reveal details of trade or war involving Becan, Tikal, and Teotihuacán.

The effects of Teotihuacán on the lowland Maya may never be fully known, but no one can doubt they were profound. The glory of the "Abode of the Gods" came to an abrupt and violent end around A.D. 600. Given the interwoven fortunes of that city and those of the Petén Maya, many archeologists feel that the consequences were unhappy for the successors of Stormy Sky. For the years between 582 and 673, not a single dated monument has been identified at Tikal—or at other centers.

Whatever the reasons for this "hiatus," the Maya would endure. As David Freidel of Southern Methodist University reminds us, "The remarkable thing is not so much that they survived, but that they came back even stronger than before."

Maya archeologists are lucky. Not only do they have the informative remains of a talented and literate people with which to work, but a vast body of other information as well. The histories and myths of colonial times, along with the legends and rituals of the present, have told us much of the Maya mind. Despite discrepancies, exasperating gaps, and many, many changes, the picture is one of remarkable uniformity.

One can, for example, see obvious links between a 16th-century narrative of the highlands and a scene on a vase made in the lowlands a thousand years before; or between the phonetic rendering of a Tikal hieroglyph and a phrase uttered last week in Chamula, Chiapas.

With little variation by region, but more consistently in the past than the present, the Maya mind saw its world as a flat square layer upon which people lived. At its four corners—the cardinal directions—stood the Bacabs, the bearded gods who held up the skies. Below them, standing in the Underworld, four corresponding Pahuatuns steadied the earth. Each direction and its gods were intimately associated with colors: red for the east—the most important direction, black for the west, white for north, and yellow for south.

In the very center of the earth stood the Tree of Life, the ceiba. Its roots reached into the Underworld, and its towering foliage brushed the heavens. The color associated with "center" and the ceiba was blue-green, *yax*—that also of jade, water, new corn, and all things precious.

The great tree connected two very different supernatural realms. The skies were arranged in thirteen layers—six steps up and six down, terraced as in a pyramid—each related to gods of varying rank and aspect, mainly good. Dominating them all was Itzamná, or Lizard House, the supreme being of sky and earth to many Maya. His four aspects, the double-headed iguana dragons, framed the heavens.

The Underworld had nine levels—four steps down and four back up. This realm was one of dread and terror, bounded by rivers of abomination and choked with the stench of blood and rotting corpses. Innumerable evil gods presided there, among them the Jaguar God of the Night, whose spotted hide symbolized the starry sky.

Each day was defined by the passage of Kinich Ahau, Sun-faced Lord, on a journey that took him through all the layers of the sky and the Underworld.

Those Classic Maya priests in charge of keeping up with such matters counted the daily passage of Kinich Ahau in terms of two important cycles of days. These formed the basis of the calendar inherited from their Preclassic forebears.

The first of these, the Sacred Round, was 260 days long. It was made up of the mathematical combination of 13 numbers —1 through 13—and a set sequence of 20 different day names. These Sacred Rounds had been repeating over and over again since the beginning of time.

The second cycle was almost a real year as we know it. Exactly 365 days long, it

included an ordered chain of 18 "months" of 20 days each, with a short final period of only five days. These years, too, had been repeating since the beginning.

These two cycles were locked together like meshed gear wheels, so that each day could be named in terms of *both* the 260- and the 365-day cycles. As any Maya mathematician could tell you, such a combination could only recur every 18,980 days.

For the ancient Maya, the naming of the days, and the reckoning of the number of them that had passed—by means of the Long Count— were not mere mechanisms. Each day number, each name, and each month had its own immutable associations with good, bad, or indifferent fortune. Thus time itself, for the Maya, became an arena for the battles of fate.

Amid the tedium of numbers, a certain poetry pervades the Maya concept of the universe. For example, in one tradition Moon was a young woman named Ixchel, patroness of weaving and childbirth, and there are many stories of her. One, told by the Mopan Maya of Belize and published by the late Sir Eric Thompson, I find particularly touching.

One day as she was weaving, the story goes, Moon was seized from her aged father by Sun. The irate old man shot Sun with his blowgun. Moon fell into the sea and shattered. Tiny fish came to her rescue and patched her with their silvery scales. Then, each holding in his mouth the tail of another, they wove themselves into a net and tried to lift the girl to Sun, but in vain. Instead, they left Moon in the sky, where she still tries to overtake her lover. The fish became the Milky Way.

As an archeologist, I am keenly interested in knowing what the past was like. Too often, the numbering of potsherds or the many other indispensable tasks of the profession obscure the people behind it all. We shall never know all the human dramas that must have been enacted time and time

Treasures from Tikal bespeak the grandeur of a lost civilization. A tomb opened in 1963 contained the superb mosaic mask below—broken into 174 pieces, now restored. This funeral mask of jade, pyrite, and shell covered the face of a Maya noble buried about A.D. *527. Above, glyphs on a lintel fragment—carved more than a thousand years ago—record a notable reign. In the right-hand column, the second glyph from the top refers to the ruler known as Double-Comb, whose vaulted tomb lies beneath the Temple of the Giant Jaguar. The lintel, hewn from sapodilla wood, crowned a doorframe there.*

again during the Maya past. We can, however, go cautiously beyond the hard data of artifacts and attempt to recapture some of those lost times. Let's take May 8, 682, a day in the Late Classic Period at Tikal.

The eastern horizon slowly reddens as Lord Sun prepares once again to emerge triumphant from his Underworld passage. From the house compounds and the clusters of modest pole-and-thatch dwellings begin the sounds of dawn—barking dogs and the rhythmic click of *mano* stones against *metates* as women begin grinding breadnuts for the day's tortillas. The acrid smoke of wood cook fires hazes the clearing as men, shadowy forms in the half-light, begin the long walk to their fields.

It is time for planting. The gathering of clouds suggests a prosperous rainy season that will not only nourish the plots of corn, beans, squash, and chili peppers, but also fill the plaster-lined ravines, now nearly dry after the long winter.

Downtown, Lord Sun lifts majestically above the treetops and illuminates the sides of the brightly painted temples in the North Acropolis. Nearby, just inside the doorway of a red stucco-covered building, an elderly priest sits on a wooden stool before a low cedar table. The coarse matting of the door-curtain has been tied to one side to let the morning light in.

Before the old man lie the tools of the mathematician: A smooth wooden plaque is scored with black slash-marks depicting the scheme of the 365-day year and its divisions. A worn screen-fold book—an affair of lime-coated bark paper bound in wood and deer hide—lies closed at his side. It contains page after page of bar-and-dot combinations and columns of hieroglyphs for the day and month signs—convenient multiplication tables for reckoning the cycles of Venus, moon periods, and the mechanics of the Sacred Round. A nearby shelf-rack holds other such books: lists of names, texts of prayers, and prophecies.

Within easy reach on the far side of the table lies a long polished wooden box on four pedestal legs. It is special, a gift of the priest's middle son, now a master carpenter. The box is divided into three compartments, each containing a set of carved wooden "counters." The longish ones, painted black, represent fives; the small brown cubes, ones; and the pellets of white shell, zeros. Working with these on the grid scored on the box lid, the old priest can add, subtract, divide, and multiply—into the billions if he needs to.

Today, the old man has already calculated, Lord Sun has completed 1,386,000 passages to reach the Long Count date 9.12.10.0.0. This day, according to his reckoning, is also 9 Ahau of the Sacred Round and 18 Zotz of the 365-day year.

The priest has checked his calculations twice, but he is an exacting man, and there is no room for error. The heat of morning brings beads of sweat to his forehead. He wipes them away with a paint-spattered cotton rag, and opens the prized box once again. The small counters click on the wood as the old man manipulates them on the grid. His calculations are correct.

The day is a good one, for it marks the end of exactly half a katun. That alone makes it worth noting. And the 9 Ahau is special as well, for nine is one of the good-luck numbers. Its patron, the youthful celestial serpent god, coupled with Ahau, one of the personalities of the Sun, should counterbalance the association of nine with the Underworld. Eighteen, the priest muses, is neither good nor bad, for its coupling—death and the young god of the corn—links opposites of equal strength.

The room becomes stifling, and the priest rises stiffly and steps outside to the shade of the terrace fronting his quarters. He steadies himself against the cool stucco of the doorjamb, and his perspiring hand leaves a brief dark stain.

The sun is higher now, and some of its rays pierce the clouds, making patches of light on the plaster of the Great Plaza.

Scaffolding and thatched shelters fringe the open space and, already, people are beginning to fill the areas that will give the best views of the ceremony.

Four days ago, on 5 Cib 14 Zotz, a new ruler, Double-Comb, had been inaugurated. He was the heir of the Sky dynasty, still revered even though its power had waned sadly since the death of his venerated ancestor Stormy Sky.

Through auspicious fortune, Double-Comb had been able to arrange the date of his accession to the rule of Tikal precisely 13 katuns—93,600 days—after the inauguration of the great Stormy Sky. The priests had deeply appreciated the coincidence of time. Today, Double-Comb's accession would be reinforced by the celebration of the half-katun end and its good auguries.

Maybe now, thought the old priest, the times of trouble would be over. Perhaps, he hoped, the sculptors could even begin carving stelae. None of those now living at Tikal ever had, for the last monument had been erected more than a century ago.

As Lord Sun approaches the highest level of the sky, preparations for the ceremony are complete. Wives, children, and retainers of the Tikal elite stand in the shade of one of the shelters. Some of the women are in long white gowns, others in elegant wraps of many colors. Everyone present wears something black as well—homage to Double-Comb, for one of his honorific titles is West Ruler.

Visiting emissaries and out-of-town cousins of the Sky family crowd another choice viewing stand. The ruler of Calakmul, the nearest Maya capital, wears a brilliant cape of yellow feathers in honor of his city and its mythical association with the south. People from Naranjo are present, too. Rumor has it that one of the Sky women has been promised in marriage to the Naranjo throne. She will, the gossips say, leave Tikal in about a hundred days.

The god impersonators, sweating profusely in their grotesque trappings, line one of the stairs at the foot of the North

More precious than gold, jade marked high status for the ancient Maya. With infinite patience, craftsmen carved elegant figures and glyphs on a variety of jade ornaments. Above, two delicately sculpted plaques reveal the supreme skill of the lapidary. Below, distinguished Mayanist Tatiana Proskouriakoff of Harvard University examines the inscription on a broken bead. Renowned for her studies of architecture and art, she discovered patterns that linked the baffling Maya hieroglyphs with scenes in sculpture—a research breakthrough proving that glyphs recorded historic events.

Acropolis. The four among them who wear different colored papier-mâché opossum masks represent the world quarters. Another has taken the role of the number Ten. The wooden skull in his headdress glistens white in the sun.

All the men ache. This morning, in the innermost chamber of the central temple of the acropolis, they purified themselves by piercing various parts of their bodies with stingray spines and other holy implements, and let their blood spatter onto strips of paper arranged in pottery plates. The impersonator of the death god wears his blood-soaked paper behind his headdress.

Assembled in a corner of the plaza, the orchestra shifts restlessly in anticipation of its cue. Three of the group hold long wooden trumpets tied with black ribbon; one trumpeter has a conch shell, its incised glyphs made vivid by red cinnabar. Other men sit alertly before drums of various sizes, holding beaters made of deer antler. Behind them stand men with turtleshell rattles, and four with pottery flutes.

here the crowd has left an open lane at the west side of the plaza, an attendant raises his hand as he sights Double-Comb's procession. A child, who had brought a last-minute drink to one of the flute players, darts back into a crowd of frantically beckoning women, and the emphatic beat of the music begins.

In the lead come four men with giant parasols made of basketry and bedecked with rare plumage. Others follow with tall banners of blue, red, and yellow cloth. Three subrulers, clad in the jaguar pelt of nobility, bear wooden carvings of the long-nosed god with the serpent foot—insignia of the Sky lineage. Behind them, carefully in step, come the litter bearers. They carry the heavy polished wooden sedan chair roofed with green plumage and holding the young ruler. A long procession follows—minor nobles, warriors, and others who enjoy honor at Tikal. All proceed slowly as the music continues. The head of the procession stops before the North Acropolis stairway, before the red temple that hides the tombs of Stormy Sky and his predecessor. The new ruler is assisted from his sedan chair by two courtiers.

The old priest, meanwhile, has moved forward to stand near the portable throne draped with jaguar pelts. He places his left palm on his shoulder in formal greeting to the brilliant entourage.

Double-Comb's slight body is heavily weighted with jade jewelry and the intricate beadwork in his chest ornament, and he pauses to assure his balance before climbing the five steps to the throne. Another attendant awaits him there with the towering headdress of quetzal feathers and the painted countenance of Lord Sun. With practiced dignity Double-Comb eases himself onto the throne and accepts the headdress. An actor, selected for his unusual height and garbed in the spotted skin and mask of the Giant Jaguar, quietly takes his place upright behind the throne.

Now the silence is broken only by coughs, bird sounds, and the rustle of costumes as thirteen dancers move from their stations near the old red monuments and assemble in the space vacated by the sedan-chair bearers. They stand ready to impersonate the divine regents of all the katun intervals elapsed since the inaugural rites of Stormy Sky.

The old priest, drawing his cues from a book, directs the chant of litanies to the holy thirteen, then to the death god and the young maize deity as patrons of this day. The dancers begin their shuffling movements, perspiring heavily, for now the real heat of the day is at hand, and the rattling of the dry seed-pods tied to their legs paces the beat of the orchestra.

Smoke begins to creep from the dark doorway of the red temple memorializing Double-Comb's distinguished ancestors. Four days ago, as the accession ceremony approached its height, forty men had assembled for an important task. With ropes

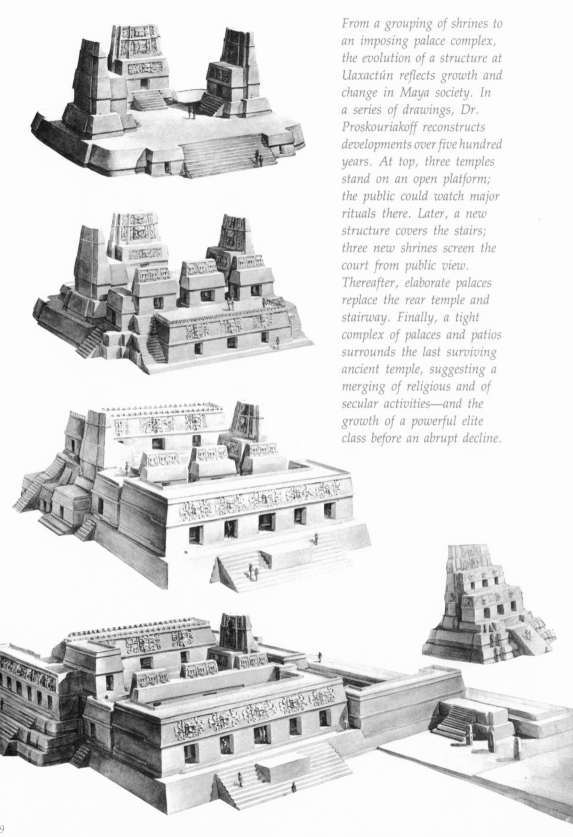

From a grouping of shrines to an imposing palace complex, the evolution of a structure at Uaxactún reflects growth and change in Maya society. In a series of drawings, Dr. Proskouriakoff reconstructs developments over five hundred years. At top, three temples stand on an open platform; the public could watch major rituals there. Later, a new structure covers the stairs; three new shrines screen the court from public view. Thereafter, elaborate palaces replace the rear temple and stairway. Finally, a tight complex of palaces and patios surrounds the last surviving ancient temple, suggesting a merging of religious and of secular activities—and the growth of a powerful elite class before an abrupt decline.

and log skids, they had hauled the great broken stela depicting Stormy Sky—the monument carved 236 years before—up the staircase and into the rear chamber of the red temple. Now, as the incense smoke pours into view, the crowd knows that the completion of the stela ceremony has confirmed Double-Comb's accession to power.

Prayers, dancing, music—these have ended. The old priest sprinkles copal into a clay brazier dedicated to the next half-katun. The young king rises; he also makes his offering to the future. This ends the formal rites, and the crowd begins to disperse. The priest will find a group to supervise the cleanup tomorrow, for already Lord Sun approaches the jaws of the Underworld. The priest watches the departure of Double-Comb, then walks slowly across the empty plaza to return the book to the rack near his table.

aya civilization reached its zenith in the Late Classic Period. This phenomenal achievement was largely one of the elite class—a group that Dick Adams estimates comprised only about 1 percent at centers like Tikal.

How big were such places? The reasonable estimation of population numbers at any given point in time, on the basis of remains that span centuries, is one of the most difficult in archeology. William Haviland of the University of Vermont believes that Tikal, at its Late Classic height, contained some 40,000 inhabitants. Coincidentally, almost exactly that many tourists now visit the great ruin each year.

William Folan, with whom I worked at Cobá, knows well the problems of trying to take a census for an extinct city. "For one thing, no one knows how extensive most of the ruins really are," he points out. "Even the most famous sites, like Chichén Itzá, are very imperfectly known. The downtown areas have been thoroughly mapped—the house mounds out in the bush, usually neglected."

Willie, with two skillful Maya helpers, Nicolas Caamal and Jacinto May, made a careful count of the low mounds in selected sample areas of Cobá. Their findings suggest a population about equal to Tikal's.

"But try to figure out which mounds were contemporary," Willie continues. "Even with minimum sampling, it's a long and expensive job. Besides, not all these mounds were dwellings. Some were probably cookhouses; others were temporary shelters in cornfields. We don't know the size of an average Maya family in Classic times either. Recent studies of the modern Maya give figures ranging from 3.5 to 5.6. With a site the size of Cobá, all these factors make one very big problem."

Excavations by Mexico's Instituto Nacional de Antropología e Historia, under the direction of Norberto González Crespo, have just begun to reveal this huge site.

The four major clusters of architecture that define "downtown Cobá" are interconnected by wide raised *sacbeob*, stone causeways that also join Cobá with outlying groups of buildings and with other sites—one of these 62 miles away.

Willie Folan and I see Late Classic Cobá as an important regional capital of the northern lowlands, perhaps the nucleus of a large and active trade network that connected the interior with the east coast. Mexican archeologists Antonio Benavides and Fernando Robles have made a thorough study of the vast roadway system, and come to the same conclusion.

Cobá closely resembles its counterparts of the Petén in *(Continued on page 73)*

In the heart of the so-called Labyrinth, a temple at Yaxchilán, the author explores the narrow chambers with Juan de la Cruz, guardian of the site for 30 years. Above their heads, high stone walls converge layer by layer in a corbeled arch. An innovation of Early Classic Maya architects, the corbeled arch limits the width of a structure but permits an impressive height.

Limestone carvings capture the life and times of ancient Yaxchilán, famous for its handsome lintels worked in stone. With a soft brush and fresh water, Mayanist Ian Graham cleans one block of a recently exposed hieroglyphic step, where two dwarfs watch a ball player in action. His brush touches a series of glyphs that record huge numbers—perhaps, he jests, "immense and improbable scores." Above, two glyphs from a limestone lintel—a full-figure monkey and the profile of a god—express portions of a single date, equivalent to February 11, A.D. 526. Glyphs on a lintel carved 183 years later (opposite) refer to fire, sacrifice, and Shield Jaguar the Great, an illustrious ruler of Yaxchilán. The scene portrays a bloodletting rite: Shield Jaguar holds a torch above a kneeling woman as she pulls a thorned cord through her tongue—a purifying sacrifice deemed pleasing to the gods.

eneath the rain-forest canopy that shelters the ruins of Yaxchilán, graduate students from the University of Texas visit a small vaulted structure with Juan de la Cruz. Traveling by canoe to study river transportation in the Maya region, the students stopped at Yaxchilán, situated along a large bend in the Usumacinta River. Selective clearing at Yaxchilán has freed many buildings from the grasp of jungle growth. Below, Mexican archeologist Roberto García Moll, responsible for much of the clearing work at the site, measures a stone ball-court marker while his assistant records the data. String grids serve as a reference guide for numbering and locating sections of the court. Overleaf: Thundering waters of the Budzilhá River plunge over massive boulders into the Usumacinta as two members of the University of Texas team paddle past the falls. Winding northwest from the Guatemala highlands to the Tabasco coast, the Usumacinta provided an important artery for the exchange of trade goods and ideas among great ceremonial centers of the ancient Maya.

ALL BY N.G.S. PHOTOGRAPHER OTIS IMBODEN (INCLUDING OVERLEAF)

N.G.S. PHOTOGRAPHER OTIS IMBODEN (BELOW AND LOWER RIGHT); MUSEO NACIONAL DE ARQUEOLOGÍA Y ETNOLOGÍA DE GUATEMALA (LOWER RIGHT)

As Lord Sun ascends from the underworld of night, the haunting ruins of a massive temple cast a shadow across Tikal's Great Plaza. Known as the Temple of the Giant Jaguar, it stands over the vaulted tomb of Double-Comb—one of Tikal's greatest rulers. Graves of the distinguished dead contained offerings such as the effigy incense burner below, found in a fifth-century tomb. Overleaf: Restored ruins proclaim the ancient grandeur of an immense and populous city. Beyond the towering Temple of the Giant Jaguar, dense jungle conceals the remains of a metropolis that covered 50 square miles in the heart of the Maya world.

N.G.S. PHOTOGRAPHER JOSEPH J. SCHERSCHEL (OVERLEAF)

architecture and sculptural style. An unusual match-up in dated inscriptions may clinch the connection: for 9.12.10.5.12, or August 28, 682. This day has no cosmic significance, such as the end of a katun. Yet it is not only recorded on Cobá Stela 1 but also at Naranjo, 250 miles to the south. At the Petén site it commemorates the marriage of a Naranjo ruler with a woman from nearby Tikal—and, perhaps, the beginning of a new dynasty.

"Sexploitation, in a sense, was very much a part of ancient Maya politics," says archeologist William Rathje of the University of Arizona. "The 'export' of women for marriage into ruling families of distant centers must have helped to cement trade relations and consolidate alliances among the regional polities.

"Women were important and honored among the Maya elite. Indeed, some may have actually ruled at important centers like Naranjo and Cobá."

Warfare and raiding were significant among the Classic Maya as well. Becan suggests this, as do the bound captives of sculpture. The famous murals that Giles Healey found at Bonampak in 1946 confirm it. There, one entire wall portrays a frantic battle in the jungle—a turbulent scene of white-eyed warriors, shields, spears, and chaos against a backdrop of dark green. Another shows the victor in triumph.

By analyzing emblem glyphs and their distribution among Late Classic centers, Joyce Marcus of the University of Michigan has found hints of extended sovereignty.

Maya warfare unfolds on the walls of a three-room temple at Bonampak, where artists portrayed ritual preparations, taking of captives, and victory. At left, one prisoner pleads for mercy before a triumphant ruler. Rendered with striking realism, and well preserved, the murals offer a rare glimpse of Maya royalty in action.

She thinks the smaller eighth-century centers, at least in the southern lowlands, may have been dominated by four great capitals. Naturally, Tikal was one; Copán, far to the southeast, another.

Of the third, Calakmul, we know very little, except that its ruins held almost 150 stelae. Many of these have lately been stolen, so we may never have the privilege of knowing Calakmul's history as recorded by the Maya who lived there.

And the fourth is Palenque.

I and many others regard Palenque as the most beautiful and evocative of all the Maya ruins. It lies on a narrow shelf of land against the forest-cloaked escarpment of the Chiapas highlands. Below it, the lush green coastal plain of Tabasco stretches northward to the Gulf of Mexico. From a distance, Palenque's buildings appear as tiny jewel casks gleaming whitely on their graceful pyramids and platforms. In contrast to the buildings of Tikal or Copán, those of Palenque seem possessed of a unique grace and lightness.

"The architects were true masters here," Paul Gendrop told me once at a conference in Palenque. A member of the University of Mexico's architecture faculty, he has made a special study of their work. "They discovered an important secret of construction. Instead of keeping the upper facades of the temples as vertical, they made them slant backward—at the same angle as the slant of the corbeled vaults inside. This gave them a lighter structure, which allowed wider rooms and much larger doorways. At Tikal, many of the rooms are so narrow they hardly seem worth the trouble of building them; the walls are sometimes twice as thick as the rooms are wide. Here at Palenque, just the opposite is true."

In one way, the architectural geniuses of Palenque helped immortalize their own work: The wide overhanging eaves of the buildings protected the graceful bas-reliefs in stucco that decorated the facades below.

"There's simply no parallel to these panels in the Maya area," says Merle

Greene Robertson, who has recently completed the laborious task of accurately recording the exquisite tracery. "They not only show scenes of myth and history, they serve to remind us just how richly Classic Maya buildings were decorated. Fine stone masonry was only the beginning."

Even among its neighbors near the Usumacinta—Bonampak, Piedras Negras, and Yaxchilán —Palenque is unique. Its rulers erected no stelae, hallmarks of the Classic Maya. Instead, its gifted sculptors carved huge panels in low relief, often illustrating their long texts with ritual scenes. These panels were set into the rear interior walls of the principal buildings.

Three such panels, containing a total of 617 glyphs—one of the longest of all the Classic texts—grace the huge building called, appropriately, the Temple of the Inscriptions. It was here that the most spectacular discovery in the history of Maya archeology was made.

In the spring of 1949, Mexican archeologist Alberto Ruz Lhuillier stood in the dark rear chamber of the temple. He was not, of course, the first visitor to stand in the room. Frederick Catherwood and John Lloyd Stephens had spent hours here sometime in 1840 cleaning and drawing the central hieroglyphic panel; and so had Alfred P. Maudslay half a century later, when he made molds of the inscription. If they or anyone else noticed the details that Ruz saw, none pursued it.

The floor, Ruz observed, was not finished with stucco as in most Maya buildings, but with carefully fitted flagstones. One, in the rear room, bore a double row of round perforations, plugged with stone "stoppers." Ruz wondered why. Curious, he began to clear the area of debris.

It was then, he reported, "that I found the cigarette butt of the criminal—the architectural detail that gave a certain clue: the walls of the temple continued beneath the floor...." There was something below, and to reach it someone must have moved the perforated stone from time to time.

Ruz and his workmen dug downward beneath the flagstones. Just below, they came upon a huge stone crossbeam. Six feet farther, through hard-packed rubble and clay, they found the straight edge of a step—a concealed staircase that led below, into the heart of the massive pyramid.

"So difficult was the work—the breaking up of the rubble packing and the lifting out of the stones with ropes and pulleys," Ruz recalled later, "that in the first season's labor, we got only 23 steps down —about eight steps a month."

Working from late April to July each year, Ruz and his crew kept to their task. By July of 1950, they had gone down 46 steps, and reached a stone landing where the vaulted tunnel turned 180 degrees and continued downward. By the end of the 1951 season, the crew had gone 13 steps farther.

"By then we knew we were close," says Ruz, "for we were only about ten feet above the level of the plaza outside."

Late May of 1952: The excavators came across a wall of stones, and a cache in a carefully mortared hollow made in the rubble. It contained three painted plates, jade beads, two ear ornaments, and a huge pearl. Beyond lay another wall and a level corridor. It took another week to clear this and the rude crypt, containing five or six skeletons, that the workers encountered. Suddenly the corridor ended; but in the final clearing at the north wall, one of the workmen's crowbars sank into emptiness. Widening the opening revealed a triangular stone, eight feet high and five wide, against the corridor wall. Ruz pressed his face against one edge of the slab, put a light through, and looked into the void.

"To my amazement, out of the shadow arose a vision from a fairy tale.... First I saw an enormous empty room that appeared to be graven in ice, a kind of grotto whose walls and roof seemed to have been planned in perfect surfaces, or an abandoned chapel whose cupola was draped with curtains of stalactites, and from whose floor arose thick stalagmites like the drippings of a candle. The walls glistened like snow crystals and on them marched relief figures of great size. Almost the whole room was filled with the great slab top of an altar, on the side of which hieroglyphs painted red might be distinguished, while on the upper surface only the fact that it was entirely carved could be made out."

Three days later, Sunday, June 15, 1952, Ruz and his colleagues turned the big triangular stone aside and descended the five steps into the room.

"I entered the mysterious chamber," Ruz writes, "with the strange sensation natural for the first one to tread the entrance steps in a thousand years. I tried to see it all with the same vision that the Palenque priests had when they left the crypt; I wanted to efface the centuries and hear the vibrations of the last human voices beneath these massive vaults. . . . Across the impenetrable veil of time I sought the impossible bond between their lives and ours."

The huge carved slab, made of the fine yellowish-white limestone that the sculptors of Palenque reserved for their most important works, was in pristine condition. Twelve by seven feet, it depicts the figure of a man reclining on the glaring face of an earth monster. Below it, and reaching up to embrace the figure, are great fleshless jaws. Behind and above the human figure rises a tree, doubtless the sacred ceiba. Atop it perches a huge bird. Celestial symbols frame the composition, and a row of 54 glyphs extends around the sides of the slab.

This great carving lay upon an even larger stone—a bulky rectangular piece estimated to weigh around 20 tons—which rested on four carved pedestals. A tiny hole that Ruz drilled into one side showed it to be hollow. The carved slab, then, was not an altar as he first believed, but the lid of a great sarcophagus.

Raising the slab was one of the most laborious tasks of all, and also one of the most exciting.

Greatest Mayanist of his day—1898-1975— Sir Eric Thompson consults one of his works, A Commentary on the Dresden Codex, *in the library of his home in Ashdon, England. His studies of ancient Maya hieroglyphic writing made him famous. His fifty years of field work and scholarship have helped dispel much of the mystery surrounding the rise and fall of Maya civilization.*

Initial Series introductory glyph

9 baktuns

16 katuns

4 tuns

1 uinal

1 kin

7 Imix

Glyph G

Glyph F

Glyph D

Glyph C

Glyph X

Glyph B

Glyph A

14 Zec

*An Initial Series
or Long Count date*

birth

accession

capture

Event glyphs

Bird Jaguar

Jeweled Skull

Woman of Tikal

Name glyphs

Palenque

Dos Pilas

Yaxchilán

Emblem glyphs

Juan Chable, a master mason and an old friend of mine, hastened the work by his expertise. "Down there in the tomb," he told me, "we didn't know if it was night or day—and we didn't care."

Below the five-ton lid, a fish-shaped cover stone lay flush with the polished top of the sarcophagus itself. Two plugged perforations in this last cover let the archeologists pry it up. Below, in a red-painted sepulcher, lay the poorly preserved remains of a tall and robust man.

He rested, fully extended, with all the precious trappings of Maya royalty.

Jade disks from a diadem lay on the head, along with the collapsed fragments of a polished jade mosaic mask, and ear ornaments engraved with hieroglyphic texts. A wide band of tubular jade beads covered the chest, and other necklaces were made of beads in the shape of tiny flowers and fruit. A jade bead lay inside the mouth; ornate rings had graced all the fingers. Near the left foot lay a jade statuette of the sun god.

Maya glyphs yield more and more information as scholars recognize patterns—glyphs for events, names, places. They can read the inscription at right, from Lintel 8 at Yaxchilán: On the day named 7 Imix 14 Zec, the ruler Bird Jaguar captured a man called Jeweled Skull. Day names refer to two concurrent cycles, the 260-day Sacred Round and the 365-day year. "This date," says the author, "can be equated with our May 7, A.D. 755. I reconstructed the complete or Long Count version of it (opposite) to show how the Maya time record works. The Initial Series glyph introduces it. Time units go left to right, reading downward: the baktun, 144,000 days; the katun, 7,200 days; the tun, 360 days; the uinal, 20 days; the kin, or sun, 1 day. Each unit has its coefficient, the number to multiply it by. Then comes 7 Imix. Glyph G identifies a Lord of the Night; the next seven refer to the moon. The last is 14 Zec. It adds up to 7 Imix 14 Zec—the passage of 1,412,661 days since a starting date that must be mythical. This is how scribes recorded any important day."

(READING ORDER HERE, DOWN EACH COLUMN IN TURN, MATCHES THAT ON LINTEL 8, WHERE CARVED FIGURES SEPARATE THE COLUMNS OF GLYPHS.)

ALL DRAWINGS BY GEORGE E. STUART

Who was the man buried in such splendor? David Kelley of the University of Calgary and Floyd Lounsbury of Yale read his name glyph as "Pacal," or Shield. This phonetic translation matches another version of the name—the picture of a shield. Meanwhile, Peter Mathews of Yale and Linda Schele of the University of South Alabama, who have collaborated with Floyd Lounsbury to reconstruct a king list for Palenque, place the birth of the man in the Ruz Tomb at 603. He lived, they agree, for 80 years before his death and interment in 683.

Alberto Ruz, now director of Mexico's National Museum of Anthropology, stresses different evidence. To his study of the hieroglyphs, he adds a series of examinations of the bones by physical anthropologists. These indicate that the man in the tomb died around the age of 40.

"First, I will refer to the man in the tomb simply by his birthday, '8 Ahau,' because I am not satisfied with any of the tentative phonetic readings for his name,"

he tells me. "I would place his birth at 655 and his death at 695. This fits the evidence of the skeleton exactly."

This disagreement stems partly from the interpretation of dates on the sarcophagus lid. There are 13 of these, but none are Long Count dates. Two, however, are "Period Ending" notations—in this case, the ending dates of katuns. For all practical purposes, such dates are as good as Long Count dates, because they recur only once every 18,720 years. The remaining eleven can be tied to these Period Endings; an event glyph identifies one as a birthday.

Ruz believes that all of these dates—which include his readings of 655 and 695—refer to events in the life of the ruler buried here, but not necessarily in chronological order. Floyd thinks that nine of them record the death dates of some of the ruler's ancestors, whose portraits appear on the sides of the sarcophagus. Moreover, he thinks these dates are in chronological order controlled by the Period Endings.

"If we don't take the Period Endings as controlling," says Linda Schele, "we're disregarding what we know about the Maya calendar. And that would leave us ignoring a statement by the Maya themselves on the life span of a very important figure."

Thus the matter stands, in its own right a significant example of method and progress in Maya studies.

Alberto Ruz expressed its goal when he said to me, "No matter what we disagree on, we are all after the same thing: We want to know all we can about that man in the tomb. None can deny that his reign must have been one of the greatest in all the ancient history of the Americas."

Whenever I can, I make a pilgrimage to the Temple of the Inscriptions, and carefully make my way down the damp slippery steps into the close warm air of the lower corridor. A doorway of iron bars now protects the entryway to the tomb; and Pacal's mortal remains rest, as before, in the sepulcher beneath the ornate cover stone.

It is here that all the Maya notions of death and rebirth seem to come together as one. Palenque itself, as the westernmost of the great Classic Period cities, must have borne intimate associations with black and the Underworld. The ancient name of the place, as yet undeciphered, appears in the emblem glyph ninth in line on the visible edge of the sarcophagus lid. Here, only dimly recognizable in the half-light, its main element is a vulture.

In contrast, the color of Pacal's inner sepulcher is red, the color of East, the direction of the symbolic daily rebirth of Lord Sun. Filling the room, the superb carving of Pacal places him squarely in the great cosmic cycle halfway between earth and the Underworld—a passage that duplicates that of Lord Sun, in which death *is* rebirth. In this holy place, one can only feel great awe, and abhor any disturbance of the honored dead.

Swift-growing vegetation shrouds the ruins of Palenque in an 1891 photograph by Alfred P. Maudslay. "I am only an amateur, traveling for pleasure," he once said; yet for 13 years he led

expeditions through the Maya area to record the remains of its civilization before time destroyed them forever. Above, a view of the Palace defines the condition of fragile stucco reliefs on stone piers. Such excellent photographs, detailed drawings, and plaster molds of stone carvings serve in restoration work as well as in archeology. What began as a "journey of curiosity" culminated in authoritative volumes that guide Maya scholars today.

If Pacal did live to the age of 80, he would have been ruling Palenque on the day of Double-Comb's accession at Tikal, and he would not die until nearly a year and a half later. The overlapping reigns of such powerful men, along with Shield Jaguar the Great at Yaxchilán and others, can only suggest the splendor of the Late Classic Maya world.

At Tikal, the reign of Double-Comb fulfilled the good omens of its beginning; it seems to have been the greatest of a dazzling age. Archeologist Christopher Jones, who has concentrated on these years, concludes that Double-Comb "presided over a renaissance." New stelae were indeed set up; a great new pyramid-temple rose over the tomb of Stormy Sky.

Double-Comb himself died about 731, having ruled for half a century. He was buried under Tikal's Great Plaza, in a vaulted chamber aligned with Stormy Sky's grave. His own memorial stands over it, at the very center of ancient Tikal's activity: the great Temple I, the Temple of the Giant Jaguar. Chris Jones describes it as "slender rather than ponderous, elevating rather than elevated, and, most of all, beautiful."

Four other great shrines, memorials to Double-Comb's immediate successors, would rise at Tikal and thrust their soaring roof combs above the forest in a symbolic flowering that would precede the twilight.

The lives and deeds of Pacal, Double-Comb, and their contemporaries are just beginning to be known. Already, however, they offer a compelling story. No one has done more to bring them to light than the distinguished Mayanist Tatiana Proskouriakoff, and it is she who explains their significance. They "remind us that Maya culture was neither static nor monolithic." Now its development, often considered a gradual process, appears as "a series of violent struggles and abrupt interactions, which are the essential elements of the drama of history." The best symbol of Maya culture is not the stela, but the ceiba tree that survives the storm.

Crowning a terraced pyramid at Palenque, the Temple of the Inscriptions possesses a serenity that belies the awesome secret it concealed for more than a thousand years. Beneath the temple—named for the gracefully carved glyphs on its inner walls—lies the sumptuous tomb of a seventh-century ruler. His name "Pacal" or Shield comes from readings of the glyphs below. Above, a jade mosaic death mask that covered his face matches the stucco head found beneath his sarcophagus.

MUSEO NACIONAL DE ANTROPOLOGÍA, MEXICO CITY (ABOVE);
DRAWING BY DAVID S. STUART

N.G.S. PHOTOGRAPHER OTIS IMBODEN

*O*ut of the shadow arose a vision from a fairy tale," wrote Alberto Ruz Lhuillier (below) when he discovered the splendid tomb beneath the Temple of the Inscriptions. Directing excavations at Palenque in 1949, Ruz found a secret staircase under the temple floor. After four seasons' work clearing the rubble-clogged passage, he reached the burial chamber of the ruler he calls "8 Ahau." A five-ton limestone sarcophagus lid (opposite) nearly filled the dark crypt. In exquisite bas-relief, it shows the fleshless jaws of an Underworld monster reaching toward a half-reclining man—probably the dying ruler.

Cleared and partly restored, ruins at Palenque nestle in forest at the edge of the Chiapas highlands. The Temple of the Inscriptions rises beyond the Palace complex with its broad stairways and unique three-story tower. Maya architects attained technical and esthetic brilliance at Palenque, where buildings adapt gracefully to the contour of the land. Unexplored mounds, choked with jungle growth, stretch for seven miles along the forested ridge behind the temples— a hint at the magnitude of a once-dazzling center. During the seventh and eighth

NATIONAL GEOGRAPHIC PHOTOGRAPHER OTIS IMBODEN

centuries, Palenque flourished under the rule of Pacal and his descendants. Kan-Xul, second son of the mighty Pacal, assumed power on June 1, 702. Overleaf: Kan-Xul's accession ceremony, inside the Palace. Enthroned among family members and priests, he accepts a sacred jade headdress from his eldest son, while his wife and a younger son present painted god effigies. Behind Kan-Xul, an oval stone tablet depicts Pacal's accession; glyphs on the throne record accession dates. Such carvings supplied portraits and details of costume and ritual for this painting.

THREE

The Blending of Worlds

By George E. Stuart

*Rattlesnake columns (in silhouette)
and a Chac Mool ceremonial figure guard
an entrance to the Temple of the Warriors
at Chichén Itzá, in Yucatán. Invaders
known as Toltec built it after* A.D. *1000.*

"YUCATÁN," wrote Diego de Landa around 1566, "is the country with the least earth I have ever seen, since all of it is one living rock. . . ." Anyone who knows the northern peninsula would readily agree, and probably add that it is among the most monotonous landscapes on earth.

As third Bishop of Yucatán, Landa knew the country well. As the first to write in detail of its people from the outsider's viewpoint, he stands as the ultimate stranger to the place; he embodies the confrontation of two worlds totally alien to each other. Yet, even as Landa wrote, the Maya had already known six centuries of strangers and invaders. The very monotony of the land stands in contrast to the turbulent story that unfolded here in Postclassic times.

This northernmost part of the Maya area begins in the gently rolling terrain of Campeche and Quintana Roo. It rises into the Puuc, a low range of hills, then spreads into a vast stony plain before vanishing into the sea. The forest that covers this land diminishes in height from south to north. Near Mérida, it is a gray-green haze of brambles and thorns where even the ceibas are shorter than their Petén counterparts. Indeed, the northwestern country that Landa knew best is virtually a desert.

There are no rivers here. But underground, the hidden movement of water has carved great caverns in the porous limestone. And, like the ancient cities built of the same stone, the shell of bedrock gives way in time. When the collapse reaches the water table, it forms *cenotes,* or natural wells—almost the sole sources of water for this ever-thirsty land.

Today, this is the home of the Yucatec Maya, largest group of all the living Maya. Here, they say, live the *balaamob,* guardians of the forest, and the *aluxob,* elf-like beings who constantly play exasperating pranks on people. On moonlit nights, one must be wary of the *Xtabay,* the beautiful seductress who waits beneath ceiba trees to lure passing men to their deaths.

The land has an astonishingly rich past,

for the Maya have lived here continuously since early Preclassic times. Even today, ruins outnumber living towns. Sylvia Garza de González, of Mexico's National Institute of Anthropology and History, is directing the Yucatán Atlas Project, a comprehensive mapping of archeological ruins in the state. So far she has catalogued some 850. She and her colleague Edward B. Kurjack and their assistants are still counting.

"Aerial photography is most useful here," she told me recently as we studied some large glossy prints, "because the bush is so low. Henequen fields under cultivation help, too. There's hardly an area free of ruins. We find new ones every month."

I gained my first impressions of Yucatán in 1958, when the late E. Wyllys Andrews IV hired me to map the ruins of Dzibilchaltún. For years, in the comfort of home, I had read descriptions of sites like Chichén Itzá and Uxmal. I had seen photographs of their spectacular buildings and complex facades, and the serene manicured plazas full of browsing tourists. Dzibilchaltún, as I quickly found out, was heaps of overgrown rubble.

I saw it first in February, at the height of the dry season. The dense bush appeared more gray than green. I learned to my dismay that trailside twigs were too often hung with dark glistening beardlets—colonies of tiny ticks that, once attached to the trouser leg, quickly spread to the most unreachable parts of the body, dug in, and itched for weeks. From my Maya helpers, Felipe Ayil and Isabel Cem, I soon learned not to swing my machete at a *subin* tree. Its large hollow thorns were inhabited by tiny stinging ants that would shower down upon anyone who inexpertly clanged a blade against the hard slender trunk. I learned, too, to distinguish the rustle of an iguana from the light crackle of ants on the forest floor, and to move quickly away if spiders fleeing a colony of ants appeared suddenly at the base of the tripod that held my survey transit.

Late in 1958, I had begun to plot in the massive platform mounds—what we called the Palace Group—near the Cenote Xlacah at the site's center. I hoped to find remains of a wall or, with luck, an intact corner that I could plot onto the map sheet.

The rubble heap I was searching was a fallen building of what is called the Puuc style of architecture. Known from Late Classic and early Postclassic times, this style takes its name from the area of its best-preserved sites—Uxmal, Kabah, Labná, Sayil. Even in collapse, Puuc architecture can be recognized by its mosaic facades and its veneer masonry. Its smooth wall and vault stones don't actually "work" like those of Tikal or Palenque. Instead, they are merely facing elements backed by a load-bearing core of rubble and concrete.

As I pondered my jumble of stones, trying to imagine what this building had looked like, I noticed a straight row protruding above the leaves and dirt—an element of the foundation, intact.

Carefully I scooped away the dry grainy dirt and old snail shells, and saw what even my untrained eye recognized as carving. The first stone bore a skull in low relief; those flanking it were carved with crossed interwoven bones. Excitedly I continued. More stones, smooth; another skull-and-bone set! At the time, the sheer pleasure of discovery, plus my spotty acquaintance with Maya architecture, obscured the significance of my find.

Only later could I appreciate its meaning. That skull-and-bone motif comes from Central Mexico—"Mexico," of course, referring to non-Maya country to the west. Moreover, only now, in the light of patiently accumulated ceramic evidence, do the varied styles of architecture offer clues to the story of change and conquest.

Joseph W. Ball of San Diego, who concentrates on this material, sees Puuc architecture as distinctive in three important respects. One is the inclusion of Mexican elements. Another is the dating, which places these non-Maya elements in Yucatán as early as A.D. 770. Another is the technical virtuosity of the buildings.

When intact, their facades are wonders of artistic achievement. They are mosaics of worked stone ornament, carefully planned and clearly mass-produced. They offer a bewildering array of motifs: thatched houses replicated in stone, panels of delicate latticework, intertwined serpents, human figures, and—most striking of all—the great stone masks, often superimposed in towering sets, with long curving noses protruding at corners and over doorways.

Most subtle of these buildings is the Palace of the Governors, so called, at Uxmal. Anyone who has seen its western facade glow in the cinnamon light of late afternoon can see why Joe Ball calls it "Mesoamerican architecture's finest moment."

If alien ideas appear in the stones of sites like Dzibilchaltún and Uxmal, who brought them? Most archeologists would say the Putún, or Chontal Maya. These people lived on the Gulf Coast plain around the mouth of the Usumacinta River. Traders by nature, with contacts deep in Central Mexico, they appear in colonial chronicles of the Maya as the Itzá—"foreigners who speak our tongue brokenly."

The presence of the Itzá in Yucatán, then in the Petén, would not only transform Maya life in the north but also would help upset the delicate balance of the Classic world to the south, and destroy it forever.

Between A.D. 800 and 900, Classic Maya civilization of the southern lowlands broke down and vanished. Richard E. W. Adams calls this "a demographic, cultural, and social catastrophe in which elite and peasant went down together."

In the grim reality of the disaster, the eternity paced by the gods of the Long Count must have seemed an unusually cruel reminder of something that simply could not be. These gods, too, died in the collapse, with the traditions of thought that created them.

The sequence of the calamity appears in the final Long Count dates carved in the

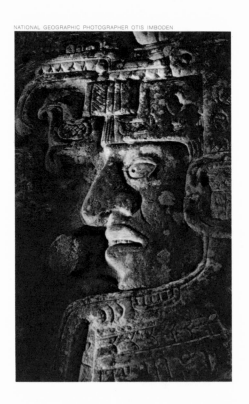

Alien in feature but clad in Maya finery, a ruler glares from a damaged stela at Seibal. This city on the Río Pasión grew powerful in Late Classic times; apparently invaders from the north had taken control of it as early as A.D. 830. Seibal's last dated stela marks the year 889. By then the collapse of Classic civilization had begun; an age of turbulence would follow. Forest claimed cities in the south; highland towns fortified themselves; foreign rule came to Yucatán.

declining centers: Piedras Negras, 795; Palenque, 799; Bonampak, 800; Quiriguá, 805; Tikal, 869; Uaxactún, 889.

That sequence creates a pattern. The earliest signs of trouble appear on the fringes of the lowland Maya area; the latest, in its very heart. Apparently, trouble came with an invasion of strangers, and the best evidence for them appears on the monuments carved at Seibal. This, ironically, is the Pasión River site where the first settlers of the Petén had come.

"Foreigners" on the Seibal stelae wear Classic Maya regalia, but they have non-Maya faces; some have mustaches. They seem to have come from the Puuc area and taken over Seibal by 830. Some traits on the Seibal carvings imply invaders from the Gulf Coast of distant Veracruz as well.

The invaders became the elite of Seibal. Over a few decades they erected its most imposing and elegant buildings. This prosperity would endure till the last stela was set up sometime near A.D. 900.

Invaders alone, however, did not cause the Classic Maya collapse. They may only have hastened it, for they appear as opportunists preying on a world already well on the road to irrevocable disaster.

The Late Classic Maya world contained the seeds of its own demise in the form of severe internal stresses. Population was one. According to geographer B. L. Turner, parts of the southern heartland were sustaining nearly 400 people per square mile—an exhausting burden for the most talented farmer. Drought that apparently began around 850 did not help matters.

Malnutrition and related childhood diseases may have contributed to the rapid decline. Frank P. Saul of the Medical College of Ohio-Toledo, who studied human bones and teeth from Late Classic burials, has found strong evidence of this, as well as a high incidence of syphilis or yaws.

Other dangers, many archeologists feel, lay in an ever-widening gulf between the elite and the common people, and in increased warfare.

William Rathje of the University of Arizona sees a general pattern of trade failure. He points out that sites like Tikal, in the heart of the Petén, lie where natural resources of any trade or sale value were, to say the least, limited. Thus their economic links with the fringe areas were always vulnerable to political change. All they could offer in return for necessities like salt or obsidian were craft products—and ideas.

"At first," says Bill, "Petén sites like Tikal were able to produce what I call a Barbie Doll cult complex based on their own local cult items. When consumers purchase a Barbie Doll, they do not buy one doll. They purchase into a whole system of optional but related sets of clothes and furniture for Barbie, friends and relatives for her, and clothes and furniture for Barbie's friends and relatives."

Barbie's outfits, Bill reasons, are like Tikal's "range of interrelated cult items—pottery and other portable cult paraphernalia, an exotic writing system, stela-cache dedication systems." If you have some items, you feel you must get others; but they are luxuries. "In the climate that preceded the collapse, this sort of thing simply wasn't enough to guarantee survival."

The causes of the Classic Maya collapse are obviously complicated and, as yet, not completely understood. Its consequences, however, are unmistakable in the archeological record of the southern lowlands. The death of the Long Count was matched by the cessation of the stela cult. Construction stopped. Farmers gave up intensive crop-raising techniques. An estimated population of three million declined to 450,000

Alfred P. Maudslay works in his room in the so-called Nunnery at Chichén Itzá in 1889. His quarters gave him comfort and a sweeping view. Yet in time he found that "ghostly grandeur and magnificence" became "almost oppressive."

in less than a century. These pathetic survivors moved into the crumbling chambers of the old palaces as their world ended.

Often my thoughts have returned to Dos Pilas and the fallen stela that Ian Graham, Otis Imboden, and I helped lift from its resting place on the jungle floor. Its date of 711 placed it squarely in the most splendid era of Classic Maya civilization. But in the momentous changes that extinguished the bright flame of the Maya Classic, Dos Pilas fell with the rest.

I'm still haunted by that great dark stone, and frequently wonder how long it stood after the people left. Perhaps one century, perhaps five. Then the roots of the huge trees that had begun to fill the terrace must have touched its short, buried base. It may have tilted just a little at first, then more, until its center of gravity passed the point of no return. Perhaps a heavy rain softened the ground for the last act. In my mind's eye, I can see the monument, dark with rain and streaked by moisture, bowing slowly forward through a tangle of vines, thumping hollowly on top of the altar before it, rocking heavily, then coming to rest in the quiet forest.

Between the town of Huehuetenango and Guatemala City, the cool pine forests cloak a highland arc of incredible beauty. Here and there the sloping ground encloses deep lakes, and the symmetrical cones of Guatemala's great chain of volcanoes stand against the sky like a painted backdrop. Far below the rocky soil lie complicated systems of fault lines that often cause the land to tremble.

Throughout the Classic Period, these highlands were occupied by Maya-speaking peoples—ancestors of the Mam, Cakchiquel, Quiché, Pokomam, and others.

"We know very little of highland cultures during the Classic," laments Richard E. W. Adams. "About half a dozen dominated the rest, and those apparently consisted of small ceremonial and elite residential centers surrounded by relatively dense populations. You find all these sites on the valley floors. After about A.D. 1000 there must have been a 'time of troubles.' Most communities suddenly move to new locations on defensible ground, usually on the tops of ridges or mountain spurs. And these sites are fortified."

Iximché is just such a site. Its ruins lie on a wide pine-covered ridge between deep ravines, by the modern town of Tecpán.

Surviving chronicles of the Cakchiquel Maya say that this was their last capital. Founded in 1470, it endured until 1524, when the cruel and genial Pedro de Alvarado burned it and placed its people under the mailed fist of Spain.

The three principal plazas of Iximché are surrounded by low stone platforms. These once held the residences of the rulers. Fragmentary frescoes show the style of Postclassic Central Mexico—an influence that seems to have permeated the Maya world by this time. Excavations here have yielded anthropomorphic vessels for burning incense, severed human heads, and ornaments of imported metal—a composite revelation of this turbulent period.

When I last visited Iximché, an earthquake had broken the great church at Tecpán, and cracked the pyramids and platforms of the older ruins.

As I made my way toward the ball court, I heard shouts and laughter. Curious, I climbed the stone platform that surrounds the playing field. Boys on a school outing were playing soccer with rules improvised for the unusual setting. As the ball bounced in and out of play on the stone ledges that flank the court, I thought that this game must have some resemblance to those that took place here 500 years ago.

Then, as throughout 2,000 years of civilization in Mesoamerica, the sacred game—played with a rubber ball by individuals or teams—was one of the most important forms of ritual activity. The game assumes cosmic meaning in one of the greatest epics of native American literature.

The story of the Hero Twins comes to us in the Popol Vuh, or Book of Counsel, the creation myth and national saga of the Quiché Maya. Its poetic narrative was written down in Quiché in the mid-16th century, and fortunately a copy was made by Francisco Ximénez, parish priest of Chichicastenango in the early 1800's.

The drama begins in a ball court in the Guatemala highlands, where the brothers 1 Hunahpú and 7 Hunahpú are engaged in a hectic game. Unfortunately, the noise of play bothers the lords of Xibalbá, the Underworld. The brothers are summoned below, defeated by the gods 1 Death and 7 Death, and sacrificed. The head of 1 Hunahpú is hung in a calabash tree.

Soon, the daughter of an Underworld lord passes the tree, and the severed head spits into her hand. She becomes pregnant, is expelled from Xibalbá, and seeks refuge above with the mother of the dead victims. She gives birth to twins, Hunahpú and Xbalanqué, who grow into handsome youths, highly skilled at both the blowgun and the ball. In time, the Twins return to the court where their father and uncle began their fatal encounter with the lords of Xibalbá. The commotion of play disturbs the lords, who issue a second challenge.

The Hero Twins then begin their epic journey through the realm of dread and horror, a journey that all Maya souls must make after death.

Hunahpú and Xbalanqué descend stone steps through hills and down steep ravines. They float on their blowguns across running rivers of blood and abomination. They reach a crossroads where four paths match the world-direction colors. Taking the black road, the Hero Twins send a mosquito ahead of them. The insect bites the assembled lords of Xibalbá, making them cry out in pain and astonishment. They reveal their names, and thereby weaken themselves. But many ordeals lie ahead.

In the House of Gloom, the Twins are given the impossible task of keeping cigars lit all night. They affix fireflies to the ends

Motifs of myth, a demon bat and a young lord playing the sacred ball game evoke the great legend recorded in the Popol Vuh, or Book of Counsel of the Quiché Maya. Twin brothers, expert in the game, arouse the envy of two gods of death who challenge them to a match in the Underworld. The mortals lose, and die in sacrifice. By a miracle, the maiden daughter of the death god Blood Chief bears their successors, the Hero Twins. They grow to manhood —and mastery of the ritual game— in this world. Again the death gods send their challenge. Now the Heroes survive all the ordeals of Hell, including a night in the dreaded House of Bats. They win the ultimate contest of the ball court, and achieve immortality. Their victory enriches the world: Now they are Sun and Moon.

of their cigars and delude their guards. They best the lords of Xibalbá in a ball game, then pass in triumph through the House of Knives, where the gnashing of obsidian blades can be heard in the dark. In the House of the Cama Zotz—the Killer Bats—the Twins sleep inside their blowguns. One is killed, but soon revived by miracle on the ball court.

Now the Hero Twins become magicians. They slash each other apart and become whole again. Asked to perform the same trick on the dread lords, they leave them dismembered, ascend from the Underworld in triumph, and take their places in the sky as the Sun and the Moon. Their uncle and father—who had become the Morning and Evening Stars—are finally and thoroughly avenged.

The journey of the Hero Twins contains ideas of death and rebirth depicted on the great sarcophagus lid at Palenque. Michael D. Coe of Yale, in his magnificent pioneer study of Classic vase paintings, demonstrates that many of the scenes described in the Quiché poem are actually shown on the funerary vessels.

"Many vases show the Hero Twins themselves," notes Mike. "Others show the Killer Bats with disembodied 'death eyes' on their wings. I feel that most, if not all, of the painted Maya vases show Underworld scenes. The story of the Hero Twins, of course, only gives us a bare hint of what must have been an extraordinary set of traditions connected with the Underworld and its many dread gods."

I never fully realized the pervasiveness of this story until one evening when I was talking with my friend Jeffrey Wilkerson of the University of Florida at Gainesville.

"Once, in 1975," Jeff told me, "we were excavating up in the Huastec area of Veracruz. One dark night—a night of new moon as I recall—the men on my crew came to me for cigars. I asked them why. Know what they said? 'We're going hunting in the woods. We have to smoke cigars so the Lords of the Night will not harm us.'"

As the ultimate myth of Maya triumph over adversity, the story of the Hero Twins should have inspired the Postclassic people of northern Yucatán.

"This epoch has been given loaded labels like Postclassic and decadent," says archeologist-and-art-historian Arthur G. Miller, whose main interest lies in its mural paintings. "I think the culture of the times belies such terms—at least in Quintana Roo, where I've been working. To me, it's one of the most exciting and dynamic times in all of Maya prehistory."

Arthur's point is well taken. Maya culture of Postclassic times clearly differed from that of Tikal and Palenque. There, gazing at the lofty temples and dark chambers, we sense a life of high art and intellect and pomp and pageant. In cities like Chichén Itzá, Mayapán, and Tulum, there is a feel of the secular, the warlike, and, most of all, the eminently practical.

Not surprisingly, change marks the method of recording time. The Long Count had died; an abbreviated system replaced it. This "Short Count" used only the notation of the *katun*, the 7,200-day period roughly equal to 20 years. These katuns were named for the day on which they ended. Because of the mathematics of the calendar, this day was always Ahau, last of the 20 day names in the 260-day Sacred Round. Its number would vary from 1 to 13. Thus the period said to have ended in A.D. 1204 was Katun 8 Ahau. It was followed by Katun 6 Ahau, ending in 1224.

For the Maya, some katuns meant good luck while others were decidedly unlucky. Katun 8 Ahau, for example, was a period of fighting and political change. Therefore the wise expected events to repeat themselves; and in the hands of those who chronicled Postclassic events, history and prophecy became interchangeable. The resulting documents are exasperating now, for the events were complicated anyway, particularly at Chichén Itzá.

At "Old Chichén," buildings in the Puuc manner reflect occupation in the ninth and tenth centuries. Then, according to a series of katun histories called the Book of Chilam Balam of Chumayel, a wave of Mexicanized peoples called the Itzá came to this site around A.D. 987, at the ending of a katun. They were accompanied by Kukulcan, the Feathered Serpent.

Kukulcan—or Quetzalcoatl, as the Aztec called him—is one of the most important figures of Mesoamerica. Central Mexican chronicles mention him as priest-ruler-god of Tollan, or Tula, capital of an empire based in the desert fringe north of Mexico City between A.D. 800 and 1000. According to the chronicles, the Toltec excelled all others at the arts of war and craftsmanship. In fact, by the time the Spaniards came, virtually every civilized culture in Mesoamerica—including highland and lowland Maya—claimed descent from them.

But Toltec history was as turbulent as the period it dominated. About A.D. 987, the priest-ruler Quetzalcoatl left Tula, made his way to the Veracruz coast, and vanished to the east. At precisely this time, Kukulcan appears at Chichén Itzá.

The monuments of Toltec Chichén nearly duplicate those of Tula in style if not always in specifics: reclining "Chac Mool" figures; huge stone columns, finely carved; the imposing "Castillo" erected over an earlier pyramid of Mexican type. Maya-Toltec reliefs decorate the Great Ball Court, Mesoamerica's largest.

Chichén Itzá centers upon two unusually large cenotes. One provided much of the drinking water for the city. The other is the famous Sacred Cenote, to me a grim and unappealing place. This great circular hole is more than a hundred feet across; its green, scum-covered water lies some 60 feet below the precipitous rim—and no one unfortunate enough to fall or be thrown in could possibly escape without help.

"Into this well," Bishop Landa wrote, "they have had, and then had, the custom of throwing men alive as a sacrifice to the

Once vessels like that above held burning incense for the gods they still portray— probably, in this instance, the exalted Itzamná, lord of sky and earth. They also commemorate the city of Mayapán, ranking power of northern Yucatán between about A.D. 1200 and 1440. Mayapán, with some 12,000 people, had no ball court, only one major temple, but many small shrines for household worship. This cult spread the Mayapán incensario *through the region; some intact vessels and innumerable broken ones prove its popularity. The style derives from the Mixtec culture of Central Mexico; the author compares its chunky deities to "gods from the Tulum murals done in clay."*

gods in times of drought, and they believed that they did not die though they never saw them again. They also threw into it a great many other things, like precious stones and things which they prized."

Immense amounts of jade and some gold artifacts, articles of wood, copper, and rubber, have come from the well—along with balls of copal incense, and the bones of children thrown in alive to placate the Rain God. The material found here comes from as far away as Panama, and most of it dates from late Postclassic times.

The great days of Chichén Itzá and its Maya-Toltec rulers vanished in chaos toward the end of the 13th century. Tula fell about this time, and the reverberations of

this shock were felt as far as Yucatán—much as the fall of Teotihuacán centuries earlier had affected the Maya lowlands.

These years also brought Yucatán's "Trojan War," as the late ethnohistorian Ralph Roys called it. One skimpy chronicle notes that a ruler of Chichén Itzá stole the bride of one of the lords of Izamal. Hunac Ceel, ruler of Mayapán and ally of Izamal, took vengeance; he sacked Chichén. In a Katun 8 Ahau, the Itzá abandoned their city and made their way south to the deserted forests of the Petén. They made a new home at Tayasal, an island in the lake that bears their name—Petén Itzá. Much later, their descendants would tell the Spaniards the story of the stolen bride.

"A Maya vision of the cosmos" art historian Arthur G. Miller calls this late Postclassic mural from a temple at Tulum. The "sky band" holds symbols of the sun and Xux Ek, the Wasp Star or planet Venus. In this world, seated goddesses receive offerings from male worshipers. Below a jaguar-pelt band lies a watery underworld. Mexican artist Felipe Dávalos G. worked day after day for four months to record the faded, flaking original by the light of a camp lantern; then he re-created the version reproduced here.

While grass began to grow tall in the great plaza of Chichén Itzá, power in northern Yucatán shifted to the city of Mayapán. Only from Morris Jones's great map of the site can one begin to see what Mayapán was all about, and how unusual it was.

First, the wall, a novel feature in this region. Five to six feet high—a tall barrier for an average Maya man—it follows the slight undulations of the limestone bedrock for more than five miles, enclosing a great irregular oval more than one and a half square miles in area.

Twelve openings in the wall gave access to the city. There, more than 4,100 mounds—remains of houses, mostly—cluster on the highest limestone rises.

In the central precinct of Mayapán rises a pyramid made in imitation of the Castillo at Chichén but smaller and not so well constructed. Around it lie the lower courses of colonnaded buildings. The stones of the columns are crudely cut, but thick layers of plaster would have hidden the defects. Once these halls were the homes of the elite who administered a city of some 12,000 and collected tribute from their neighbors.

With a flair for eye-catching titles that matches his brilliance in analyzing Maya culture, Bill Rathje has called this culture the "Last Tango in Mayapán." Indeed, it was the final drama of a Maya story that had begun three thousand years earlier, and it illustrates well that the dominant theme of that long epic was change.

Mayapán is a strange place. There are no ball courts here, few temples. Instead, large, brightly painted *incensarios* or incense burners appear in the form of Mexican gods—and in astounding numbers. The villagers of today will tell you that they come to life at night and roam about; perhaps the Mayapán incensario is the original hobgoblin *alux*. Certainly it suggests a change from public to private devotion, at household shrines instead of great temples. Yet there was a revival of the old stela cult. In just two centuries, some 25 monuments were erected. Unfortunately, those that were carved are too eroded to be read.

In the end, Mayapán vanished in dissension and conspiracy. Katun 8 Ahau had returned, a time to hearten men seeking change. One faction of Maya lords, the Cocoms, brought in mercenaries from the Tabasco lowlands. Others resisted the move, Mayapán disappeared as a political force about 1440, and thereafter northern Yucatán fragmented into 16 petty states.

All was not chaos and war, for Yucatán has one dependable constant: salt. One of the largest deposits in Mesoamerica lies along the northern coastline, and the trade that it supported continued unabated into colonial times. Great seagoing canoes skirted the low shoreline, bringing obsidian, copper, and fine textiles of Central Mexican origin from the Gulf Coast to Yucatán, trading for salt and honey, then continuing southward to Honduras for metates and axes of hard stone.

Thus it was the sea that brought Yucatán its final prosperity. On my most recent trip to the area, I went to the ruins of the little walled coastal town of Tulum—possibly Zama, the "City of the Dawn" mentioned in Postclassic chronicles. I went before day, and awaited the sunrise at a vantage point on a low stucco-covered building above the jagged sea cliff. Venus as the Morning Star made a bright pinhole in the dark sky. This was a malevolent sight to the Maya—the uncanny Wasp Star returning from its sojourn in the Underworld—but Lord Sun would wash it away with its greater light.

I wondered if someone had been standing here about 460 years earlier—on May 7, 1518. Probably so, probably a priest watching the same interplay of good and evil in the natural world. Had he consulted his katun prophecies, he would have been deeply dismayed.

The current katun, 2 Ahau, was one of ill omen. Within less than two years—on February 25, 1520—there would begin the appalling Katun 13 Ahau. That, said the books of oracle, would bring the end of the world, when "blood shall descend from the tree and the stone, and heaven and earth shall burn."

And had the priest waited till late afternoon of that day in May, he could easily have picked out the forms of great wooden ships on the turquoise horizon.

Masks of the rain god, Chaac, cover the facade of a palace at a site called Kabah. Such rich, repetitive ornament marks the Puuc style of architecture, named for a region of hills—puuc, in Yucatec Maya. Influence from south-central Mexico may have inspired the Puuc artists.

Uxmal's huge Pyramid of the Magician catches evening light while shadow grips the Monjas, or "Nunnery," quadrangle. One of the largest of northern cities, Uxmal draws many visitors by the beauty of its buildings, considered the finest examples of the Puuc style; but

DAVID ALAN HARVEY

despite its accessibility, it has never received full-scale scientific study. From perhaps A.D. *700 to 1000 the city flourished; then a small remnant group lived there; then it lay abandoned. The rulers of Mayapán knew of it, but only as a place of vaguely remembered splendor.*

Chichén Itzá reveals its heritage of conquest in Toltec structures (right) and earlier Maya buildings. Square pillars—once crowned with masonry—in the Northwest Colonnade frame the huge pyramid called the Castillo. Identified as an ancient observatory and rounded by erosion to resemble a modern one, the Caracol shows knowledge of astronomy probably gleaned from long observation. Windowlike openings in the tower align with the sunset at spring and autumn equinoxes. Spaniards called the building El Caracol, "The Snail," because of a spiral stairway that gives access to the tower.

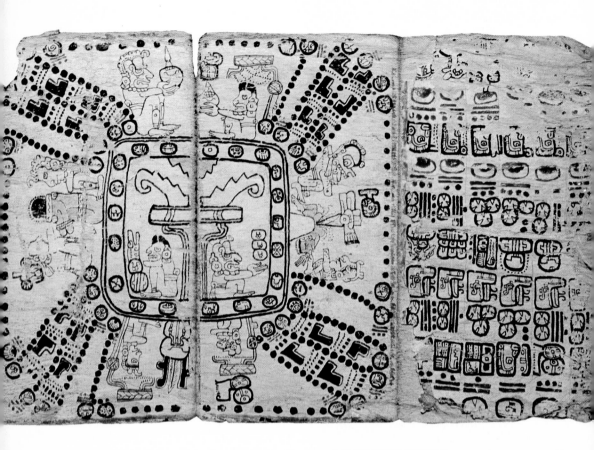

Overleaf: A scribe copies a text from the Classic Period as a servant smooths a bark-paper strip with a wooden mallet and another checks a thin white plaster coating. Folded like a screen, such coated strips make up a handwritten book, or codex. Above, pages from the Madrid Codex deal with the 260-day cycle called the Sacred Round and represent deities with such attributes as corn and incense. Only three Postclassic Maya books of undisputed antiquity have survived. The fragment at right, with other scraps, reached the scholarly world early in 1977. Experts have assessed the rendering of glyphs and pictorial details, a vague tale of discovery, and other factors. Their conclusion: This "find" almost certainly amounts to a fake.

N.G.S. PHOTOGRAPHERS OTIS IMBODEN AND VICTOR R. BOSWELL, JR.; MUSEO DE AMÉRICA, MADRID; ACTUAL HEIGHT 8 9/10 INCHES

Creased but unbroken, the sheet-gold disk below came as a crumpled ball from the Cenote of Sacrifice at Chichén. A drawing reveals its details: A Toltec chieftain, his spear bearer in attendance, threatens a Maya warrior who offers his reversed spear in surrender; between them sits a wounded Maya. At least ten such disks recorded the triumphant Toltec presence.

GOLD DISK: ACTUAL DIAMETER 10 INCHES. DRAWING BY TATIANA PROSKOURIAKOFF. BOTH, PEABODY MUSEUM OF ARCHAEOLOGY AND ETHNOLOGY, HARVARD UNIVERSITY.

At Progreso, chief port of
modern Yucatán, a fisherman brings
in a string of fresh groupers.
Fish and other seafoods supplied
protein in prehistoric times; the
Late Classic vase below proves an
artist's observation of a catfish
and of shells. Brackish lagoons
along this coast offered sources
of salt to the ancient Maya, who
traded it far inland. Ethnohistoric
evidence—Indian accounts recorded
after the Spanish Conquest—
indicates that sea lanes in this
area linked sites to the north and
west with scattered ports on the
east coast of the peninsula.
Traders traveling in large dugout
canoes went as far south as
present-day Honduras as a matter
of commercial and political routine.

DAVID ALAN HARVEY (OPPOSITE); NICHOLAS M. HELLMUTH,
FOUNDATION FOR LATIN AMERICAN ANTHROPOLOGICAL RESEARCH
FROM A PRIVATE COLLECTION

L̲ast outpost of a splintered civilization, Tulum still constitutes a landmark on the Caribbean coast. The small Castillo, barely 40 feet high from bedrock to rooftop, dominates the main plaza. At left, a workman clears the remains of a colonnaded hall—one example of the Mexican government's program to make sites attractive to visitors. From about A.D. 1200 till the Spanish Conquest, traders and pilgrims brought prosperity to Tulum and its shoddily built but brightly painted shrines. Overleaf: Seamen of A.D. 1450 beach their dugouts and unload their wares; on the largest craft a canopy shades a visiting dignitary and his consort. Women came from afar to the offshore island of Cozumel to worship Ixchel, goddess of healing and of childbirth.

FOUR

Conquest and Aftermath

By Gene S. Stuart

Proud and austere, a Guatemalan woman stands outside a church in the highland village of Nebaj. She carries her child in a hand-woven rebozo, a garment of Spanish name. Maya traditions survive in this remote area, largely unchanged from pre-Conquest times.

DAVID ALAN HARVEY

"*Mire el mar. Que bravo está hoy*—Look at the sea. How fierce it is today," he said.

I leaned forward against the wind to catch the words of my old friend Juan Chable. We stood high on the cliffs of Tulum and watched the Caribbean hurl foaming turbulence against the rocks below. A few days before, a hurricane had swept along the coast of Quintana Roo to slam destruction onto Honduras and leave a wake of chaos in a sea that still churned itself white with fine limestone sand.

Fierce it was. Menacing, ferocious, daunting. And so were the Spanish explorers who sailed from Cuba to test those same shores and find equally brave Maya warriors eager to defend their land.

In the many years that I have known Juan, he has worked with his crew of masons, helping archeologists to excavate and restore a host of ancient Maya cities—Dzibilchaltún, Palenque, and Uxmal among others. Now they worked at temples in the Postclassic center of Tulum.

The Spanish explorer Francisco Hernández de Córdoba discovered the peninsula of Yucatán in 1517. The following year a chaplain, Juan Díaz, sailed the east coast with Juan de Grijalva; later he wrote: ". . . almost at sunset we saw in the distance a town or village so large that the city of Seville could not be better or larger; and in it could be seen a very large tower. Many Indians were running along the shore with two banners which they raised and lowered, signaling us to approach; but the captain did not wish to." The impressive city he saw was probably Tulum.

Grijalva skirted the peninsula, at times landing for explorations and supplies. Near the river that he named for himself, he received gifts from the Maya. Díaz recalled, "They brought gold cast in bars . . . a beautiful gold mask, a figurine of a man with a half mask of gold, and a crown of gold beads. . . ." To the Maya, gold was a gift from the sun, though less significant than jade; to the Spaniards it meant instant wealth, prestige, and fame.

The captain of one of the ships, Pedro de Alvarado, would later sweep through the Maya highlands to conquer them for Spain. And another member of that Grijalva expedition, Francisco de Montejo, would return to conquer the Yucatán Peninsula. In 1519, Hernán Cortés visited Cozumel Island on the coast, but then he sailed on westward across the Gulf of Mexico to conquer the Aztec and gain riches beyond Renaissance dreams.

At Cozumel, Cortés learned of two countrymen, Gerónimo de Aguilar and Gonzalo Guerrero, survivors of a 1511 shipwreck. Aguilar, formerly a lay brother, was serving the Maya as a slave. He greeted his countrymen joyfully, and joined Cortés as an interpreter in the Aztec conquest. A Spanish chronicler reported, however, that Guerrero "was already converted into an Indian and was married to an Indian woman. He had his ears mutilated and his tongue cut in sacrificial fashion, and had his body painted. . . ."

Later, Francisco de Montejo learned that Guerrero was in service to the Maya lord of Chetumal as a military leader. Guerrero refused Montejo's invitation to join the Spanish conquerors, and later led Maya warriors against them. In his detailed account of the conquest, historian Robert S. Chamberlain considered the value of his role: "Some Spaniards openly attributed their military reverses to Guerrero's genius."

This brave leader "died as he had lived." He took a hand-picked force of Maya troops to Honduras by canoe to aid the Indians there. After leading his contingent against Pedro de Alvarado's soldiers, he was found dead on the field, "dressed, painted, and ceremonially lacerated like an Indian."

In 1526 Montejo had received permission from the King to conquer Yucatán. He, his son, and nephew found that the Maya there were split into rival militaristic groups. Chamberlain listed their weapons: "strong bows, obsidian and flint-tipped arrows, lances and darts with fire-hardened or stone points and swords of hard wood in which razor-sharp flakes of obsidian were set. They wore thick cotton armor which was so effective that the Spaniards themselves used it."

The Maya soon found that in the open field, Spanish weapons and horses would overwhelm them; they turned to guerrilla and siege tactics. When they built defense works, said Chamberlain, they showed "a high degree of engineering skill, a good eye for terrain, and excellent strategic sense." The last major groups, in the eastern part of the peninsula, were not officially conquered until 1546—24 years after Cortés defeated the Aztec—and some were never really subdued. The lord of Chetumal expressed their defiance; asked for a tribute of foodstuffs, he promised "fowls in the form of their lances and maize in the form of their arrows."

Cruelties against the Indians often shocked priests who accompanied the Spanish soldiers. In a letter to the Crown, a Franciscan missionary lamented the acts of an officer at Chetumal: "Tying them to stakes, he cut the breasts off many women, and hands, noses, and ears off the men . . . and he threw [women] in the lakes to drown merely to amuse himself." The Indians "fled from all this and did not sow their crops, and all died of hunger."

Though Spanish armies swept through Yucatán bringing widespread death and famine, the Maya never united against them. Traditional hatred rankled among the lowland Maya rulers, especially the Cocom family of Sotuta and the Xiu of Maní. The Cocoms had maintained their "empire" for some 250 years through marriage alliances with subordinate states. They called themselves the true Maya lords and looked upon the Xiu as foreign interlopers. Around 1446 the Xiu had burned the Cocom capital, Mayapán, killing all of the ruling family except for a prince who was on a trade journey to Honduras. About 1536, hoping to alleviate drought and famine, the

Xiu decided to sacrifice slaves in the sacred well of Chichén Itzá, and asked the Cocoms for safe passage through their territory.

Diego de Landa, Bishop of Yucatán, reported the outcome in his history of the peninsula: "The Cocoms deceived them by a kind answer, and giving them lodging all together in a large house, they set it on fire and killed those who escaped. And this gave rise to great wars and the locusts kept coming to them for five years so that nothing green was left."

Before the peninsula was securely theirs, the Montejos founded Campeche in 1541, named for the Maya district of Canpech. The following year, in the ruins of the city of Tihó, they built their capital. They named it Mérida, a chronicler remarked, "because on its site they found buildings of lime and stone, worked and with many mouldings as those which the Romans built in Mérida in Spain."

"Give us a lift to Tihó," Maya workmen once said to me as we climbed into a truck. It was the end of a working day in the ruins of Dzibilchaltún, early in the first season George and I were there; I thought they wanted a detour to some village.

"Can't. Sorry. We're going to Mérida," was my reply.

"It's still Tihó to us," they explained.

And Valladolid, near Chichén Itzá, is still—among the Maya—Saki.

Brutality, forced conversion to Christianity, mandatory tribute and service to foreign masters. The peninsular Maya were appalled by Spanish cruelties and inspired to frenzy by priests of their own religion. On the night of a full moon, November 8-9, 1546, they struck. In the Maya calendar it was 5 Cimi 19 Xul—Death and the End. Valladolid took the brunt of the attack, surrounded by 20,000 vengeful warriors. Neither women, children, nor Christian Indians were spared. A siege began that was not easily broken, and a pattern of rebellion began that would continue for centuries.

Maya uprisings occurred sporadically,

- Cities and towns
▲ Archeological sites
○ Populated places of archeological importance

From the coast of Yucatán, Spanish invaders spread inland after 1527, finding some allies but often meeting bitter resistance. Amid ancient ruins they founded their capital in 1542, "the very noble and very loyal city of Mérida." Maya defeat near Utatlán in 1524 had already assured the conquest of the highlands; but the last of the Maya kingdoms, Tayasal, on an island in Lake Petén Itzá, kept its independence until 1697.

but were always put down. Conquered Indians either learned to cope with Spanish domination or fled to places like Petén Itzá that were still free.

"I call these areas 'zones of refuge,' " historian Nancy Farriss of the University of Pennsylvania told me. "The Maya who went there were families or individuals, usually not whole populations, but it was a steady movement."

Mazes of paths in the bush let a family flee to freedom with all their possessions bundled onto their backs. The Spaniards complained bitterly about Maya mobility. Other Indians, in small isolated hamlets, continued living as their ancestors had for centuries. A change from Maya overlords to Spanish ones meant little or no change to them.

While the conquest of the Yucatán Peninsula progressed unevenly, that of the highland Maya came swiftly by comparison. The fall of one Guatemalan kingdom, that of the Quiché, determined the rapid collapse of less powerful states. Like the lowland Maya, they were divided by militaristic rivalries, and the Spaniards shrewdly played them off against one another. What must have been one of the most dramatic battles in all of history decided the fate of the Quiché Maya in 1524.

Pedro de Alvarado, cruel, fearsome, gallant, blond and handsome. The Mexicans called him Tonatiuh, the sun. Cortés sent him south with a Spanish army and 300 loyal Mexican Indians. Tecum—grandson of the king, honored "warrior of the mat," Captain of the Armies of the Quiché, Lord of the Banners and Staffs—heard of Alvarado's approach and prepared.

Several Quiché nobles in the 1560's wrote an account of the battle and its consequences. The delicate, fragmentary document reads in part: ". . . for seven days he [Tecum] was carried on their shoulders at Quiché [Utatlán] among the great houses; he was carried in feathers and precious stones, with black and yellow anointing, when he got his glory . . . the warriors . . . bled themselves by piercing. . . ."

The chronicle says there were so many Quiché warriors that they could not be counted. The two armies met beside a river on a plain at the edge of a pine forest. Both Tecum and Alvarado joined into battle with their men. Alvarado later wrote that the fighting was at such quarters the Indians crowded up to the very tails of their horses. The tattered chronicle continues: ". . . the head of his horse [Alvarado's] was taken off by Captain Tecum . . . Tecum was pierced . . . the trotting horses of the Spaniards in the plain . . . he was deprived [of life] in his body; thus he went down that day before heaven and the great fire-mountain [volcano]. . . ."

Tecum had dressed elaborately for the battle. He wore three crowns of gold and silver adorned with precious stones and pearls. Green iridescent quetzal feathers decorated his hair. Alvarado was so impressed he called the other Spaniards to look at their fallen enemy. They named the place Quezaltenango in memory of the quetzal feathers in his hair and ". . . because a great captain died. . . ."

The Quiché could not "count the number of companion people of Tecum who died, but the sun in the sky turned red because of the blood. . . ."

One of the Quiché authors then recalled sadly, "I was a child, a little child when it came down over me here; I was born there in the beautiful stone buildings of my grandfathers and fathers . . . the great walls and stone structures, here. . . ."

Recently I walked through that Quiché city, Utatlán, with anthropologist Robert Carmack of the State University of New York, Albany. We stood at an outpost on the edge of the ruins and shielded our eyes against the sun as he pointed to a range of distant hills.

"Alvarado and his army came from behind those hills," said Bob. "They traveled the Quiché causeway across the plain toward the city." I could almost hear the clink of Spanish armor; hear the deep rumbling hoofbeats of a mounted army; see the storm of dust they stirred, see distant darts of light reflect from metal weapons undreamed of in a Maya world.

"There, below us, that's where Alvarado sentenced the Quiché king and four other rulers of Utatlán after the battle," said Bob. "Then he burned them alive. He baptized the surviving princes and gave them Christian names. One, he named Juan Rojas.

"Over there," he gestured toward a small Maya house across the dusty road. "I want you to meet some friends of mine."

We entered a compound through a gate of poles to meet a modern Quiché family.

"Juan Rojas, his wife and children," Bob introduced us. "The same name in each generation for over 450 years." He swung their baby into the air. "And this is little Juan—the newest Quiché prince."

In the 1560's, an ancestor, Juan Rojas, helped write that story of the fall of the great city. The present family farms a few acres in its shadow, and Don Juan supplements their small income by braiding palm leaves for hats. Bob Carmack believes they still live on some of the land that once belonged to the ancestral Rojas clan. Later, we walked down a steep path to a spring that today supplies water for the family, and centuries ago had quenched the thirst of pre-Spanish Utatlán. It bubbles at the mouth of a cave whose walls are blackened with centuries of smoke from incense. Before we left, Bob told us that his own son had been born the week before.

"We named him Tecum."

While the Conquest was still incomplete, the Spaniards gained a commodity in great demand in the Caribbean islands—slaves. Packed by the hundred into holds of ships, they sailed to replace the native populations that had died by the thousand from overwork and disease. The original island peoples had

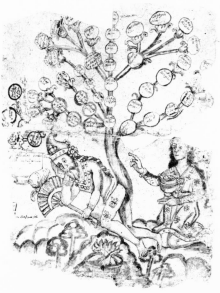

Family tree rises from the loins of the forefather of the Tutul Xiu, powerful rulers at the time of the Conquest. The founder, Hun Uitzil Chac, wears a headdress similar to the turquoise mosaic crown of the Aztec empire. His wife, lady Ix of Ticul, kneels behind him, pointing to the record of their heirs. The Tutul Xiu, of Mexican descent, claimed to have founded Uxmal—a claim that modern scholars doubt. About 1446, however, the Xiu overthrew the Cocom dynasty of Mayapán and established themselves as lords of Maní. Bitter rivalries between these two families—and Xiu support of the Spaniards—helped ensure Spanish rule in Yucatán. Drawn about 1560 by an unknown artist, this famous document employs a Biblical motif, the "tree of Jesse," to explain Xiu nobility to the Spanish Crown. Such proof of elite status often meant official favor in the early colonial period.

almost disappeared fifty years after the first Europeans arrived. Most of the exported Maya slaves came from Yucatán.

In the highlands beyond the Maya area, gold nuggets and silver ore in the rivers meant demand for labor to retrieve it. Population displacement became common.

A Cakchiquel Maya historian wrote of Alvarado's rule in 1530: "During this year heavy tribute was imposed. Gold was contributed to Tunatiuh; four hundred men and four hundred women were sent to wash gold. All the people extracted the gold. Four hundred men and four hundred women were contributed to work in Pangán [Antigua] . . . by order of Tunatiuh. All this, all, we ourselves saw, oh, my sons!"

elocation to unaccustomed climates, slaving, overwork— the destruction of many thousands of Maya was related to some purpose, but many thousands more died from something over which the Spaniards had no control—Old World diseases unknown in the New World. The conquerors brought with them smallpox, measles, plague, cholera, tuberculosis, typhoid, typhus, and malaria. The Maya of Yucatán spoke of it as a time "when the vultures come into the houses" because no one is left to tend the dead.

The first epidemics of smallpox and plague killed from one third to one half of the Indians in Mesoamerica. After a century of Spanish occupation in what is now Mexico, perhaps as much as 90 percent of the Indian population had disappeared.

By 1550 exportation of Maya slaves had virtually stopped. Forced labor disturbed many of the priests, mostly Dominicans and Franciscans, who had come to save pagan souls. Bishop Bartolomé de Las Casas left his post in Chiapas and returned to Spain to protest the treatment of Indians. The result: The Crown set limits to the worst abuses of Indians.

"We are as shocked as if an order had been sent telling us to cut off our heads," protested colonial officials. In a letter to the King, they condemned the good bishop as "a friar unread in laws, unholy, envious, vainglorious, unquiet, tainted by cupidity, and above all else a troublemaker."

Diego de Landa worried over the old Maya religious customs and beliefs, but he observed them closely and wrote an extremely valuable record of them.

"Having assembled, clothed in their ornaments, at the house of the lord, first they drove away the evil spirit as usual, then they took out their books . . . and invoking with prayers and devotions an idol named Kinich Ahau Itzamna . . . they offered him gifts and presents and burned before him their balls of incense. . . ."

In afterlife, the Maya told Landa, the good would "go to a delightful place, where nothing would give them pain and where they would have an abundance of foods and drinks of great sweetness, and a tree which they call there *yaxche*, very cool and giving great shade, which is the *ceiba*, under the branches and the shadow of which they would rest and forever cease from labor."

If Landa felt deep concern over the existence of pagan practices, he became alarmed at what seemed to him extremes of cruelty and blasphemy. The Maya had long practiced human sacrifice; in Yucatán they began crucifying children for the Maya gods. In Maní, in 1562, Christian Indian boys discovered a cave with altars, idols, and the scent of *copal* incense. Spanish priests had proof then that most of their "followers" still practiced the old religion. Many Indians were arrested and tortured; some suffered sentences of at least 100 lashes. One was Francisco de Montejo Xiu, governor of the province. Landa destroyed the idols, and burned the sacred books to the horror of the people. Tradition says this took place at the ceiba tree of Maní, the center of the world to the Xiu.

Landa himself left no reference to the scene at Maní, but acknowledged that he had destroyed "a large number" of codices: "as they contained nothing in which there were not to be seen. . . lies of the devil, we burned them all which [the people] regretted to an amazing degree. . . ."

Some of the Spaniards themselves regretted the loss "of many ancient matters," and one, in 1590, published an eloquent rebuke of the clergy's "stupid zeal."

The sacred hieroglyphs lost to them, the Maya guarded their lore as best they could. A 16th-century Spanish friar noted in Guatemala: "When old men are about to die, they pass their idols to some other old men. They bid them guard them, honor them, and venerate them, because they and those who follow their law and custom will prevail, and that the Spaniards were upstarts and must come to an end."

In 1697 a priest wrote of the Chol-speaking Lacandon in lowland Chiapas: "It grieves us to see that when the drum is beaten (which is the signal for the Catechism in the mornings and evenings), the boys and girls wish to come, but their parents and mothers will not let them. On the contrary, they send them to the fields to play saying, 'Do not go there, because if you do, you will die.' "

And among the Ixil Maya of Nebaj and other villages in Guatemala, a parish priest of the 19th century mourned the failure of 300 years; the people, he said, were "regressing toward the old barbarism. . . ."

In the chronicle of Chumayel, a Maya historian contrasts the past and the colonial present. "The moon, the wind, the year, the day, they all move, but also pass on. All blood reaches its place of rest, as all power reaches its throne . . . Measured were the days of beneficence of the sun, of the latticework formed by the stars from whence the gods look down upon us.

"There was health, devotion; there was no sickness, aching bones, fever or smallpox; no pains in chest or stomach. They walked with their bodies held tall. But the *Dzules* [foreigners] came and undid everything. They taught fear. . . . There was no longer great wisdom, nor word nor teaching of the lords. The gods that arrived here

Salvaged from a ruined church in Yucatán, this 18th-century wood carving of a Franciscan friar reflects the modest skill of a local craftsman and the religious fervor of colonial art. As the first missionaries in Yucatán, the Franciscans worked devotedly to convert the Maya to Christianity. Advocates for the Indians, they spoke out against bondage, excessive tribute, and other abuses. But they could not end oppression. The statue's scars may date from the 19th-century Maya rebellion known as the War of the Castes, when the Indians rose against overlords in church and state.

were worthless! The Dzules came only to castrate the Sun! And the children of their children have stayed with us, and we receive only their bitterness. . . ."

Nancy Farriss explains the fate of Maya leaders. "Because of their relatively small numbers, the Spaniards were on the defensive immediately after the Conquest," she told me. "They used the native nobility to rule and manage Maya populations. As the numbers of non-Indians or *Ladinos* slowly increased in time, the special treatment of aristocratic Indians declined. Finally, all the Maya were equal peasants."

Once the late Sir Eric Thompson remarked to George and me, "I've never quite forgiven the Xiu for selling out to the Spaniards. They accepted the Spaniards —and the Cocoms never did."

Throughout the colonial period, Spanish priests taught and punished; conquerors and their descendants demanded tribute and labor. Although slavery was generally forbidden, rebel Indians could be enslaved as punishment. Others became legally bound to plantations and sometimes inherited large debts when their wages were only a few *centavos*. Corporal punishment was common for such offenses as "lack of respect."

Priests and public officials gathered many Indians from their scattered farms into towns for better control of religious instruction and tribute. Many fled. Rebellions were inevitably put down, and Maya bondage continued, in fact if not in law.

Cacao, indigo, cattle, sugar—at various times plantations enjoyed booms or endured depressions. One of the first large money crops had been cacao, a currency in its own right in pre-Hispanic days, and highland Maya were sent to the lowlands to work it.

"The military phase was the first conquest," Nancy Farriss commented. "But the plantations were the second conquest. Those were the worst times for the Maya."

One official wrote of the new diseases and their effect on the Maya sent from the cool highlands to the Pacific slopes of Guatemala: "This land is a general sepulcher for all these Indians who come to it. . . ."

Ironically, diseases the Spaniards had brought killed the Indian labor essential to fulfill their dreams of wealth. Spanish colonists imported black slaves in many areas to replace the Maya for plantation labor. What had once been a proud Indian people—with their own nobles and slaves —were miserable in their oppression.

Yet many preserved their old ways, and some remained independent.

In the tangled jungle of the Petén, the refugees from Chichén Itzá had established the island stronghold of Tayasal in Lake Petén Itzá. It maintained its freedom far longer than any other Maya state.

In 1696, Andrés de Avendaño, a Franciscan who understood the Maya calendar, visited Tayasal and reminded the chiefs that Katun 8 Ahau, the katun of fighting and political change, would soon begin. He explained that the time for their conversion to Christianity had come, and they agreed to embrace the new religion at the beginning of the dreaded katun. But even before it began, a Spanish army arrived at the

Yucatecan National Guard units at Nohpop prepare for a review during the War of the Castes. Religious tensions and economic exploitation gave rise to this prolonged Indian revolt that began in 1847. Surrender of the rebel stronghold, Chan Santa Cruz, officially ended the war in 1901. Memories of the struggle remain vivid in the present-day state of Quintana Roo.

shores of the lake, built ships, and sailed to the island kingdom and victory in 1697.

Sir Eric Thompson wrote that the Itzá warriors "put up very poor resistance. It is possible they did not fight well because they knew resistance against the power of the incoming katun was useless."

Yet the Conquest was not without ironic reversals of influence. By the beginning of the 18th century, most of the people in Yucatán, including the white masters, spoke Maya as their first language.

By 1800 the depleted Indian population of Yucatán had begun to increase. By mid-century it had spiraled. Until then, haciendas occupied a relatively small portion of land on the peninsula. The rest belonged to the state or to Indian villagers who farmed the land communally. But two crops became valuable, and their worth demanded vast private land holdings and Maya laborers to work them. One was sugarcane; the other was *henequén*, sisal, or "green gold" as it came to be called.

The state sold enormous tracts of land for a low price. Ladino cattle, left free to roam, destroyed the sacred corn of the Maya as it grew in their fields. Hacienda owners increased their conscription of Indians, who found themselves indebted for life as serfs. Orphans could legally be sold as servants. For most hacienda owners, a whipping post for their Indians was as necessary as watering troughs and cool shade trees for their cattle.

In 1847 the Maya struck back, and the Caste War of Yucatán began. Nelson Reed of Washington University, St. Louis, has written its history. He notes that one Indian leader's hatred of whites was so strong that he "was simply for killing them, down to the last woman and child." One of the most successful attacks against the whites was by the Cocom villagers around Sotuta, "showing what could have been done in a peninsula-wide revolt." At one point the rebels held most of the peninsula, and the governor considered evacuating the besieged city of Mérida, but suddenly and mysteriously the enemy disappeared.

Years later the son of a Maya leader explained. "When my father's people took Acanceh they passed a time in feasting, preparing for the taking of Tihó. The day was warm and sultry. All at once the *sh'mantane-heeles* [winged ants, harbingers of the first rain] appeared in great clouds to the north, to the south, to the east, and to the west, all over the world. When my father's people saw this they said to themselves and to their brothers, 'Ehen! The time has come for us to make our planting, for if we do not we shall have no Grace of God to fill the bellies of our children.' . . . Thus it can be clearly seen that Fate, and not white soldiers, kept my father's people from taking Tihó and working their will upon it."

By 1850 the Maya had been driven back toward the east. In the refugee town of Chan Santa Cruz, a miracle gave them new hope. A talking cross appeared, urging them to fight. A man of mixed blood and a Maya ventriloquist had invented a cult that the rebels embraced with zeal. Another Indian posed as Christ on earth. Throughout the century, Ladinos and Maya inflicted and suffered massacres. An American traveler, Frederick Ober, described the impact of Indian hatred on the people of Mérida: "Every year they send a threatening message to the capital, promising to make its streets run with blood, and every year the people quake and turn pale . . . ."

An uneasy peace came in 1901 when the land of the rebel Maya was separated from Yucatán and named the Federal Territory of Quintana Roo. There are villages there today that invite white people to leave almost before they arrive.

In Chiapas another Caste War began in 1867, led by Indians of Chamula. A Maya shepherdess, tending her flock, saw three stones fall from heaven. Another Indian, Pedro Díaz Cuscat, placed them in a box. Soon they became objects of worship and "talked" to the faithful. Indians turned against the religion of the Ladinos and sought a messiah of their own. As anthropologist Demetrio Sodi Morales reports, "On Good Friday, 1868, a boy 10 or 11 years old, Domingo Gómez Checheb, was crucified, the blood removed from his body and perfumed with incense. An author of that period even suggests that the blood was drunk by the leaders of the movement."

The Indian siege of San Cristóbal de Las Casas began in 1869. They fought a battle with the white defenders, then withdrew to their mountain strongholds, from time to time attacking towns and ranches, killing everyone including women and children. By 1871 the movement lost its strength, and peace returned; but in more than 100 years only one Catholic priest has lived in Chamula, and he was asked to leave.

During the War of the Castes in Yucatán, many hacienda workers remained loyal to the whites, out of long habits of obedience and a prudent suspicion that their masters would eventually regain power. Around 1880 a henequen boom began that brought new riches to the landowners.

Once again the old pattern emerged. There were not enough Maya workmen for the land. Demand for henequen on the world market far exceeded the supply. Yaqui Indians from northern Mexico and Koreans by the hundred were shipped in as indentured hacienda workers.

In 1883, there were 333 haciendas in Yucatán; often one person owned several. Of his journey from Mérida to Uxmal, Ober wrote that he was ". . . received in a princely manner by Don Alvaro Peon, the courteous proprietor. This gentleman, a splendid specimen of manhood, cultured and travelled, is the present representative of an ancient and distinguished family, which estimates its possessions by hundreds of square leagues. In going to Uxmal, I had ridden all day, . . . nearly fifty miles, over territory once owned by his father."

Splendid, indeed. Don Alvaro Peón y de Regil, who had taken the Castilian title Count of Miraflores, lived most of his time

Despite superior weapons, Mexican troops fall in an Indian's interpretation of a Caste War battle. Contemporary accounts confirm the accuracy of such details as the use of machetes and ambush from the shelter of stone walls. The Maya rebels held most of the peninsula in 1848, forcing the whites to flee to Mérida. Later, after the arrival of Mexican regulars, the Indians, plagued by disease and famine, retreated into the forest. Sporadic fighting continued for decades, even after the "final" surrender.

I.N.A.H. CENTRO REGIONAL DEL SURESTE; PHOTOGRAPH BY OTIS IMBODEN

in Italy. On trips to Yucatán to see to his possessions, he always dressed in formal clothes in the European fashion. When he visited one of his haciendas, "Torres de Peon," with its high towers and merlons, "one of the servants would announce his arrival by playing the trumpet, exactly like an old Castillian arriving at his castle . . . in Mérida, he lived in the house with his brother, Don Pedro, another gentleman; and it is said that when one brother wanted to visit another he only did so after announcing himself through his card." A contemporary of his in Yucatán stated matter-of-factly that "One could say that he never committed an incorrectness." Also, "Since he was a gallant man he never passed up the opportunity for an amorous adventure, but only if and when it was up to his level."

As Nelson Reed summarizes a pattern: "The master, the *hacendado*, was seldom seen. He lived far away in the city, and his rare visits were like a descent from another world, a holiday when the peasants, excused from work, dressed in their best and lined up to kiss his hand."

An Indian earned 25 cents a day, paid in tokens stamped with the name of the hacienda and redeemable only in the plantation store—which also belonged to the owner.

Henequen wealth sent Yucatecan sons to be educated in Europe, built French-style chapels for the Indians to attend services, refurbished hacienda houses with fleur-de-lis murals and delicate gilt chairs.

"They had too much money too fast," a lady told me in Mérida. It could not last. The henequen boom ended in 1918 with the close of World War I. President Lazaro Cardenas enforced land reform. In the 1920's he returned 25 percent of the haciendas to the Maya. Since then, even more have come into Indian hands. An aunt of a friend of mine had 25 haciendas reclaimed from her at one time. But other reforms have been slow. A Maya could not stay overnight in San Cristóbal de Las Casas until 1965, and could not even walk on its sidewalks until 1960.

The old noble Maya names are still there in Yucatán. Many who bear them are emerging as leaders today. A distinguished teacher and a state legislator are both Xius. When I first moved to the ruins of Cobá to live for a time, my next-door neighbor, the legal delegate to Carillo Puerto (formerly Chan Santa Cruz) introduced himself and made me feel genuinely welcome. His name? Don Isabel Cocom.

On the coast of Campeche, at Siho Playa, the stone manor house of the colonial sugar plantation has been restored as a hotel. Late one afternoon I stood there at the edge of a completely calm green sea strewn with crystals of sunlight. Frigate birds and gulls lazed homeward.

Two Maya fishermen slumped low in their tiny boats slowly made their way down the coast from the direction of Jaina, the island cemetery where Classic Maya buried their dead—an island to the west, direction of death. Sailing from the Spanish colonial city of Campeche that had been Maya long before the Conquest. Sailing slowly past me toward coastal Champotón, the ancient homeland of the Itzá.

I stood on the edge of the land, limestone rocks blackened by salty surf. Now tiny waves broke softly. The sun sank lower along its path. Halfway across the horizon the refraction of its own light turned it into a stepped Maya pyramid of gold. It seemed to ride the dark blue sea a moment before evening fell—descending into the underworld and leaving the world to night—and it left a brilliant glow where it had been shining only moments before.

Worshipers face an ornate altar at the Church of San Francisco in Antigua, a colonial capital of Guatemala. Built by the Spanish—with Maya labor, exacted as tribute by the conquerors—the church became an important center for Franciscan missions in colonial days.

Solitary on a calm morning, a canoeist paddles across Lake Petén Itzá, 27 miles in length, itself a defense of the Maya stronghold of Tayasal. Isolated in almost impenetrable jungle, the island nation of the Itzá survived until 1697, its collapse completing Spain's conquest of the Maya. Overleaf: Conquistador Don Pedro de Alvarado leads his soldiers—mounted and armed with lances—in battle with warriors of the Quiché nation. Wearing a headdress of quetzal plumes, Tecum, Captain of the Quiché, raises his obsidian-edged "sword" of hardwood to strike Alvarado's horse. As a Quiché chronicle noted, "The flag bearers and valiant warriors, the companions of Tecum, forced their way [into the battle]" when the armies met in 1524 near Quezaltenango, Guatemala. Their noble leader slain, the Quiché soon surrendered, their fate resolving the conquest of the Maya highlands.

Cool shadows attract an Indian to rest in a colonnade at the Convent of San Antonio
in Izamal. Founded in 1549 by the Franciscans and built by Maya workmen, the great
Convento replaces a demolished Maya pyramid—a site chosen by the conquerors
to symbolize the defeat of the native gods. At right, Yucatecans crowd the town plaza
of Izamal on December 8 to celebrate the Feast of the Immaculate Conception, a
principal religious festival of the early Spanish colonists. On the skyline rises Kinich-
Kakmo, a Maya pyramid still significant in popular cult. There the devout finish
their pilgrimage, many climbing the steep staircase with the aid of a rope (overleaf).

DAVID ALAN HARVEY (ABOVE, BELOW, AND OVERLEAF)

Candlelight ripples on evening air—and distorts a spectator's shadow—as villagers carry a statue of their patron saint along a street in Izamal. These processions, events of general enjoyment, mark the fiesta of Santo Cristo de Sitilpech, in October. At Maní, Maya children explore the famous cave where Indians hid their holy images from Spanish authorities. Its discovery in 1562 coincided with evidence of another pagan practice: child sacrifice. As ranking official of the Church of Yucatán, Father Diego de Landa ordered public rites of penance; the sacred Maya texts were burned. Scholars still lament this loss, and Landa noted that it caused the Maya "much affliction."

ALL BY DAVID ALAN HARVEY

Mound of sun-dried henequen fiber strains a laborer as he pushes the cumbersome load along light rails—steps en route to a cordage factory. In earlier stages of harvest, a worker slices the longer leaves from the giant plant, and a crew unloads bundled leaves for the machine processing that separates fiber from pulp. Henequen flourishes in the thin soil of the Yucatán Peninsula, which now produces about half the world's supply. In the late 19th century it transformed the economy of the area—and the lives of many Maya. Owners of haciendas, or plantations, saw a rising demand for rope and twine; they turned from corn and cattle raising to this new cash crop. They acquired land from Indian communities, and sometimes secured Maya workers by money-lending, when labor never quite paid off the debt. As an American visitor said in the 1880's, the plantation owners "live a life of luxury." Maya servants attended them when they visited their lavish rural estates (overleaf).

FIVE

The Round of Life

By Gene S. Stuart

Warm in color but airy and cool in texture, a new hammock cradles Rode and Eufemia May of Yaxhachén, a village in Yucatán. Though buffeted by centuries of turmoil, the Maya remain a resilient people. Of the hammock, brought by the Spanish from the Caribbean islands, they say: "It's like sleeping in your mother's arms."

DAVID ALAN HARVEY

THE OBJECTS FOR THE RITUAL lay on a table between us: a book, a gun, a weeding blade, scissors, and three silver coins. I held out my infant son to Maria Ybarra.

She took him in her arms, saying in Maya, *"Koten, Roberto Gregorio Stuart, ten kin mentik hetzmek tech*—Come, Robert Greg Stuart, I make the *hetzmek* for you." She continued, "There are all the things I give you to grasp; you have to learn them when you grow up."

She read a prayer from the book, a Catholic missal, then placed it in his fat baby hands.

"I give you the book in order that you learn to read." Then the gun. "I give you the gun in order that you learn to shoot." In turn: ". . . the blade in order that you learn to farm . . . the scissors that you learn tailoring . . . the money in order that you may learn to earn money from your work when you grow up."

Maria helped Greg hold all the objects as she placed him astride her left hip, signifying his passage from infancy into babyhood. Then she slowly circled, counterclockwise, nine times around the table. Both Greg and Maria wore a crisp white *huipil*, or Maya dress, embroidered with designs of green leaves and purple grapes. Earlier she had fastened a small gold bracelet around each of his wrists.

That sunny afternoon in Mérida, Yucatán, 18 years ago, my son's future was assured. He would be educated, become a good hunter and farmer, know a trade, earn money. The nine Lords of the Night would protect him—with the help of the Christian church. The bracelets promised good health through his first two years; the grapes, a fruitful and prosperous life. Maria had learned the ceremony in her village, Lepán, an old hacienda near the ruins of Mayapán. No one can say how many hundreds or thousands of years it has been performed, nor when the Christian element was included. But its meaning is as powerful as its roots are deep—the survival of the Maya people.

We had a guest that day, Alfredo Barrera Vásquez, an authority on the modern Maya. At the end of the ceremony he commented, "It varies so much from village to village in Yucatán now. Some parts have been forgotten, others added."

Yet miles away, in Maya groups so isolated they know little of one another and so different in dialect they cannot converse, it also continues.

In the thick forested lowlands of Mexico's state of Chiapas, the Lacandon, most isolated of the modern Maya, show a baby what it must learn. For a boy, a man climbs a tree, clears bush, and shoots an arrow from his bow. For a girl, a woman demonstrates grinding corn, making tortillas, and what she thinks are the motions of weaving—not everyone remembers how. Then the child is placed on the hip for the first time and given a name.

Chiapas rises from the low jungles into mountainous highlands that are chill when fog rolls down into the shadowed villages. There, in Zinacantan, within an hour after birth, the midwife presents the ritual objects to the child: a *mano* and *metate,* or corn grinder, and parts of a loom to a girl; farming tools and a splinter from a torch to a boy. Then she quickly wraps the mother and child in blankets to protect the baby's delicate "inner soul."

Recently, I returned to Yucatán and attended the hetzmek of a grandnephew of two old friends, Tránsita Varguez de Ancona and Irene Varguez de Ramos, in the village of Telchaquillo, near Lepán. They are sisters; both were childhood friends of Maria. Bright sunlight held rain clouds at bay as we stood among their relatives in the Varguez family compound. The infant arrived, dressed in a yellow nylon suit. He sat in the arms of his godmother, Tránsita, as she gave him a silver coin, a notebook and a pencil, a spool of thread, and a religious picture. She placed him on her hip, then a male relative did the same. The ceremony—

cheerful and informal—was finished. No table had been laid for the ritual. No one walked in a circle. Not a word had been said; yet young Walfred Matilde Varguez Uc, no longer an infant in arms, had taken his place in the modern Maya world.

That afternoon turned into one of games and feasting. I sat with the women in the cookhouse-shelter behind the one-room thatch-roof house while we exchanged news of births, children, illness, marriage, death. The men sat apart and talked of jobs and inflation, hunting and farming. At the end of the meal as shadows grew long, the patriarch of the family, Don Daniel Varguez, eyed the dark clouds and said, "This is the first time in days it hasn't rained. Very rare, this rain in February. Summer flowers are in bloom. Everything is wet. The black bean crop has rotted in the fields. We cannot burn milpas to plant corn, and what there is to eat, the locusts take. There are millions of them this year. What can you do?" he shrugged.

Too much rain. Not enough rain. That universal age-old affliction still plagues the Maya farmer.

For two summers my family and I lived in the village of Cobá, Quintana Roo, near the eastern coast of the peninsula. There, I became fully aware of the dependence of farmers on the behavior of nature, sometimes ideal and benevolent, sometimes cruel and capricious. Despite ceremonies loyally performed for them, the gods are generous or they are not.

In 1974, the rains came before mid-June. Crashing afternoon and evening storms dumped rapid-flowing rivulets on the newly planted fields. Harvest that year was bountiful. More than enough corn to last the year. Enough left over to sell.

But during the second summer, not even a light shower had fallen by late June. Clouds built up, turned dark; and, helpless, we saw them drift to the north or eastward out to sea. The men of the village said they would not plant their cornfields if rain did not come in ten days. We waited. Hot wind

146

swept black dust through the pole walls of our house. By noon every day our heads throbbed from the heat and we sought a cool haven under our roof of thick palm thatch. Sometimes a sleek mare and her little foal with a startled scrub-brush of a mane trotted along the road; their hoofs made a hollow sound against the dust and porous limestone underneath. Jacinto May showed us his watermelon patch—little shriveled melons the size of limes.

The men began to speak of the rain god, Chaac, and plan a *Chachaac* ceremony to ask his favors. They chose a day. The village women ground corn and squash seeds for food offerings. I boiled extra drinking water, certain that after the ceremony it would rain hard and often, and my outside cooking fire would be useless.

On the appointed day a Maya priest from a nearby village arrived at dusk. Word swept through Cobá that he would let women attend the Chachaac ceremony. I was amazed, for ceremonies for rain and planting are exclusively the sacred charge of men. This was a ritual that I might never again be privileged to attend. We asked the men to suggest appropriate offerings.

"Candles, beer, cigarettes or soft drinks. A hen if you have one."

We didn't, but a village store was still open. Laden with cigarettes and Coca-Cola, George and I with our daughter Ann and sons Greg and David, followed them along a path into the high bush. It wound through ruined Maya temples and palaces and into an ancient courtyard. Dark breadnut trees, heavy with Spanish moss, circled a clearing, and there in the center stood an altar made of poles and freshly cut branches. Arches, also made of branches, stood at each of the four cardinal directions. In front of each arch was a pole, with a beeswax candle thrust into the splayed top end.

The priest was a gentle man, middleaged, and like all the northern Maya, immaculately clean in his blue work pants and orange shirt. He motioned us to place some of the cigarettes on the altar. The other

Long-time friend of the author, Tránsita Varguez de Ancona holds her four-month-old grandnephew and godson Walfred Matilde Varguez Uc after conducting his hetzmek ceremony at Telchaquillo. She gave him a coin, a religious picture, and other objects of adult use; then held him—for the first time in his life—astride her hip. This rite signifies the passage from infancy to babyhood, the beginning of growing up, the awakening of adult skills. She wears the finely embroidered huipil of lowland Maya tradition; he wears novel finery, a new outfit of yellow nylon.

offerings lay to one side. We spoke in whispers and scattered ourselves in a semicircle outside the area of the altar and arches, choosing fallen stones from the ancient temples to sit on. The priest took small gourd bowls from a plastic shopping bag. He hung some in the arches and arranged the others on the altar on a ritual bed of *chimché* leaves. One, he placed underneath, then filled them all with water.

Darkness closed our sacred clearing into a small circle of candlelight as the air calmed to solemn stillness. No one moved, no one spoke. I sat with my youngest son, David, beside the wizened roots of a breadnut tree. Near us lay a trough made from a hollowed log and covered with a sheet of plastic. The priest moved to the trough, quickly took something from it and slipped it into a gourd. At the altar he stirred the contents with a small bundle of tightly bound leaves.

In reaching into the trough he had pulled aside the plastic cover, and in the candlelight I saw a design burned deep into the wood—a cross. It was then I noticed a small brass crucifix on the altar. For a loincloth the Christus wore a skirt like the old Maya men still wear, but made of white cloth and embroidered with red flowers like a huipil.

The priest knelt on a dusty feed sack in front of the altar and began to pray. His voice was low and steady—so low that I could not hear a distinct word, but I knew that he spoke Maya and there was no need for him to speak loud, for this was a priest speaking to the rain god, Chaac, and what was happening at the moment was between them.

An assistant knelt behind him, and I thought how much like a Catholic mass it looked—a priest kneeling at an altar with his acolyte. And then suddenly it seemed to be a Catholic altar. The branches intersecting over the middle formed a dome. I realized it was *(Continued on page 173)*

To celebrate a memorable day, Tránsita's relatives and in-laws prepare a feast. This includes making tortillas, a daily chore that can take three hours. Maya women rise at dawn to boil and grind corn for the dough they will cook on a griddle or skillet over the fire. Below, a Late Classic plate illustrates the process. A woman works dough on a metate, *the larg[e] stone that holds corn for grinding under a* mano, *or stone rolling pin.*

PLATE, DIAMETER 12 1/2 INCHES, PRIVATE COLLECTION; NICHOLAS M. HELLMUTH, FOUNDATION FOR LATIN AMERICAN ANTHROPOLOGICAL RESEARCH. DAVID ALAN HARVEY (OPPOSITE)

VASE (LEFT) FROM COLLECTION OF JOHN H. HAUBERG, SEATTLE;
NICHOLAS M. HELLMUTH, FOUNDATION FOR LATIN AMERICAN ANTHROPOLOGICAL RESEARCH

Hunters of Yaxhachén set out at dawn, hoping to bag deer or wild pig and birds in the forest near Labná. Boys help beat the thickets to flush game. The dogs, prized as hunters, earn such names as Presidente, Rey, and Tarzán. Though disappearing rapidly, certain rituals still attend the hunt in parts of Yucatán. Hunters in the Puuc may stop at a cross and offer a gourd of corn gruel to the "Lords of the Hills" who might grant them a kill in their domain. A good outing will yield a stag—and the dog that found the prey gets a special share. Above, a Late Classic vase portrays the return from a successful hunt, with musicians playing conch-shell trumpets.

DAVID ALAN HARVEY

María Perfecta Ramos Varguez—fondly called "Chucha" by her Aunt Tránsita and other relatives—cuddles her pet rabbits in her arms. In addition to caring for younger children, she feeds the livestock her family raises, pigs, chickens, turkeys among them.

ALL BY N.G.S. PHOTOGRAPHER OTIS IMBODEN

In the village of Muna, children cavort outside the dry-stone wall that surrounds a lowland house, seemingly as impervious to time as to the heat and storms of Yucatán. Women draw water daily from the common well, and enjoy unhurried conversation. Though a subsistence mode of life continues, change approaches such lowland communities. Schools give instruction, but always in Spanish only; roads and electricity bring the outside world nearer. Overleaf: In their mud-chinked home at Yaxhachén, the wife and children of Valentino May Us reflect a measure of prosperity, a serene—and vulnerable—simplicity.

DAVID ALAN HARVEY (OVERLEAF)

At a family tomb, Teresa Briceño Alvarado of Oxkutzcab places flowers in observance of All Souls'. Here the dead return on the last day in October and the first in November. The living pray at sunrise, noon, and night; invite each other to delicious meals; and take flowers and candles to the graves. Eight days later, they take offerings of food, for the visitors must depart on another year's long journey. Summer, season of rains, brings special perils in Yucatán. Contaminated water seeps into wells and spreads epidemics of typhoid fever and dysentery. Mourners, among them the godfather with hat in hand, watch as the supervisor of the Oxkutzcab cemetery nails down the coffin lid over an eight-month-old baby who died of diarrhea. At left, as depicted in the Dresden Codex, the loathesome Yum Cimil—God of Death—sits on his throne of bones. Among the ancient Maya, he commanded a grudging but profound respect.

RODOLFO BRICEÑO

Maya known as Lacandon still practice
basic skills deep in the forests of lowland
Chiapas. Descended from Indians who fled
Spanish colonial efforts to relocate them in
new towns, they have borrowed little
from alien cultures—until recently. Above,
two men carve a mahogany dugout canoe
in the tiny settlement of Mensabak. They
work with ax and machete, tools acquired

more readily since the logging industry reached the forest in the 1870's. Easily steadying their dugout, two boys cross a stream at Mensabak. Tributaries of the mighty Usumacinta, abundant with fish, vein this land. The Lacandon raise corn, squash, and tomatoes in the fertile soil and hunt such diverse prey as armadillos, monkeys, and wild turkeys. Smoking a cigar of home-grown tobacco, a man fashions a wooden bird-bolt, an arrow designed to bring down a bird without harming its plumage. Now the Lacandon hunt with firearms and sell the weapons they craft to outsiders. External factors, including government policies for land use, may again rule the fate of the Lacandon. At highland villages such as Tenejapa, a shortage of arable land has prompted a migration to the Lacandon forest.

Huddled against the highland cold, barefoot as always, women of Tenejapa wait to watch a

fiesta. As in the past, they accept roles sharply distinguished from those of men.

$\mathcal{C}$arnaval unfolds in Tenejapa during the five days preceding Ash Wednesday. A major religious festival in highland Chiapas, it not only precedes the Lenten season for the clergy but also imposes special obligations on dignitaries known as cargo holders. During their one-year terms they tend the images of Christ, the Virgin, and los santos, and sponsor their celebrations. In these duties they must meet heavy expenses, but they earn the high esteem of their fellow villagers. Cargo in Spanish can mean "burden," stirring memories of the Maya gods who carried units of time with bundle and tumpline. At right, cargo holders exchange ceremonial toasts of pox, or cane liquor—a common ritual of greeting in the highlands. Called the Festival of Games by the Indians, Carnaval includes a number of stylized diversions. Below, in a hubbub of shouting, celebrants lope across a field, good-naturedly baiting a man costumed as a bull. Adding to the excitement: the beat of a deep-toned drum.

DAVID ALAN HARVEY (ABOVE AND RIGHT)

NATIONAL GEOGRAPHIC PHOTOGRAPHER OTIS IMBODEN (ABOVE); DAVID ALAN HARVEY (OPPOSITE)

W*ith banners whose flowers symbolize divinity, cargo holders of the highland village of Chamula sprint across burning thatch in a climactic rite of Carnaval. Civil officials watch from a balcony. Here Carnaval links the Passion of Christ with memories of battle, including the Caste War of 1867-1870 when Chamula rebelled against the disdained Ladino oppressors. Below, ritual assistants perfume the furled banners with incense. The lance tip of the flagstaff evokes the spear that wounded Christ and symbolizes Yahvalel Vinahel, the Sun, Owner of Heaven. This festival gives the highest-ranking cargo holders, Christ's helpers, their title* Pasión. *The villagers say of them: "When the* Pasión *walks, Christ walks; when the* Pasión *dances, Christ dances; when the* Pasión *runs, Christ runs."*

DAVID BRILL

Giant crosses mark Chamula's Romerillo cemetery. Planks, called "doors to the graves," lie

strewn by the wind. For All Souls' Day villagers deck the crosses with pine, symbol of life.

$\mathcal{S}$trong sense of community gives meaning and constancy to life in Zinacantan, in highland Chiapas. Its settlement pattern suggests ancient Maya practice: Zinacantan encompasses a ceremonial center and a periphery of hamlets. Below, a harp player in the hamlet of Nabenchauk rouses a flurry of resonant notes while his daughter embroiders a stole. Musicians—with harps, violins, guitars, flutes, and drums—invariably gather to play for the celebrants in the frequent religious festivals. While cargo holders assume duties of religion among the Zinacantecans, civil officers, serving three-year terms, take charge of secular matters. At right, elected officials in Nabenchauk hear a land dispute. Both defendant and plaintiff bring them cane liquor as tribute; then each argues his case before the seated panel. On this occasion the presidente, who wears a plastic rain cap on his hat, presides, and shares the deliberations of the two judges beside him. After harvest, a farmer winnows his grain—corn, "sunbeams of the gods," cascades from his basket.

Frolicking boys roll tires and hoops near home at Nabenchauk. In their lighthearted midst a woman labors, undistracted, at her backstrap loom. Maya sons do not join their fathers in the fields until the age of nine or ten. Thus they can amuse themselves while little girls have already begun working with their mothers. Their duties include caring for younger children and making tortillas. They also gather firewood, fetch water, and lead sheep to graze along the trails. While tending her flock, a small shepherdess may twirl her spindle or set up a portable loom to develop the skills she needs as weaver and wife-to-be.

like a Byzantine church made of branches. The four arches of the four directions were the four wings of the church. I smelled incense. Someone had thrown it onto a shovel filled with glowing embers. And then we were on our feet and the priest's voice rose strong above ours as he began in Spanish, "Hail Mary, full of grace."

I stood behind Mexican archeologist Antonio Benavides and saw his face in profile as he prayed with the priest. Pale skin, dark wavy hair, close-cropped beard and dark heavy-lidded eyes. The Spanish conqueror, Montejo, must have looked much like that when he landed on these shores and the ancestors of this very priest fought in desperation to keep the Spaniards from their land.

Our prayers continued. Finally the priest dipped his bound leaves in a gourd and scattered the now-blessed water in the four directions across the altar. We found our fallen temple stones again and rested.

The men poured some of the blessed water into a bucket of more water, mixed it with ground corn, and passed gourds of the drink to all of us.

"What is it?" asked David.

"Zacá, a holy drink—a sacred drink for Chaac," I answered.

"Oh," he said, and began to drink in short serious gulps.

The ceremony continued. As the priest prayed in Maya, young boys sat beneath the altar imitating frogs.

"Woh, woh, rana, rana," their voices rose in a plaintive cry for rain.

We chanted the Christian prayers in Spanish. "Our Father's, Hail Mary's," over and over again. Then we rested and drank another gourd of zacá. Near midnight the moon rose white and full above the eastern arch. Liquid in the trough began to make intermittent bubbling noises. It was a fermenting mixture of water, honey, and bark from a *balché* tree. Between rounds of prayers the men sometimes drank beer or shared a cigarette from the altar.

Often the exhausted priest fell asleep.

Walter F. Morris, Jr., a student of Maya textiles, shows the author a wedding huipil richly interwoven with feathers. Once this intricate technique of weaving flourished throughout Mesoamerica, but now only the women of Zinacantan practice it. A mural, painted in 1759 in a highland church, documents a changing style of headdress for men; today, streaming ribbons substitute for the lordly plumes of old.

When it was time to begin again an assistant touched his arm gently and whispered, *"Nohoch Tata*—great father."

Each round of prayers lasted forty-five minutes, and there were nine in all. At dawn the rounds were complete. But already the priest had taken out his polished sacred divination stones and spread them across the feed sack. He examined them carefully, then slowly shook his head.

"There will be no rain for Cobá."

As the sun rose, the leaves on the altar wilted, the candles burned to molten stumps, and the men prepared the feast. They placed thick cakes of corn dough, layered with ground squash seeds and marked with a cross, into a large pit lined with hot stones. They covered them with palm leaves, then filled the pit with dirt. While the bread baked, chickens bubbled in a caldron of broth, blood, and spices.

The priest's assistants and the frog boys politely served us each four gourds of balché, a gourd of Coca-Cola, then balché mixed with Coke. Waves of nausea began to sweep through me. The food was placed on the altar and dedicated to Chaac; then the first course was served: ground yellow corn mixed with bright yellow chicken feet on a banana-leaf plate. We could not stay. Of our family, only Greg remained in the clearing.

The balché had not fermented enough to be alcoholic and hallucinogenic as it is supposed to be, but it is in all its stages both purgative and emetic.

For the rest of the day I draped my cleansed soul and purged body in a camp chair while George ministered to all of us. Ann lay sprawled on the cool tile floor at the Mexican archeology camp next door, unable to move. I had found David deathly pale and exhausted beside the trail, hanging limp, with his eyes closed, knees buckled, arms dangling listlessly, and his chin wedged into the fork of a little tree. Ann and I have probably attended our last Chachaac ceremony. But Greg and young David may well be part of such a night again.

In the following days we watched the sky anxiously, hoping the prediction was mistaken. A few showers fell in late July; then rain stopped until autumn. That year, no corn grew in the milpas of Cobá.

The hot, flat peninsula of Yucatán, with its sparse rainfall, is in sharp contrast to the highlands. Highland rainfall is usually plentiful. Tall evergreens and oaks darken mountainsides. Cornfields angle so steeply that often a farmer, wrapped in mist, stands straight up on one row and his face almost brushes the roots of the stalks above him. But there, as in the lowlands, farmers grow one crop more vital than any other—corn.

"Sunbeam of the gods" they call it in Zinacantan, and treat it as a miracle gift. Like the child, corn has an inner soul. They plant it with a ceremony to the "Lord of the Earth" who sends clouds, wind, and rain. At harvest time mounds of shelled corn in the field bear a small wooden cross at their summits, and in the family compound, piles of corn in storage bins are sometimes topped with crosses.

Evon Z. Vogt is director of the Harvard Chiapas Project that has been studying the people of Zinacantan for more than twenty years. He recalls that the people have such a deep respect for corn that once, when a container of corn gruel spilled onto the floor of the project Land-Rover, a Zinacantecan passenger quickly bent down to lick it up with his tongue.

"That was clearly an act of reverence," says Evon Vogt. "And if single kernels are spilled, they're picked up immediately."

Corn serves not only as a staple of food and drink, but also as a ritual food; and kernels become a means of divination and counting. Zinacantecans still employ the ancient methods their ancestors used, planting their steep mountainside fields with a digging stick, weeding with a hoe, and harvesting by hand.

There are more than 17,000 Zinacantecans living in the village, the political and religious center, and in 25 outlying hamlets. Together these form the municipality of Zinacantan, which covers some 95 square miles immediately to the west of San Cristóbal de Las Casas, Chiapas.

The narrow dirt road to the central village winds steeply into a hidden valley and crosses an old stone bridge. There, near sunset, women drive flocks of sheep home from their pastures. Near the central church, men gather to chat. Their clothing is a swirl of color: red and white pinstripe tunics, pink from a distance and tasseled with brighter pink, light blue neckerchiefs, and cascades of bright ribbons hanging from their flat straw hats. They call a low mound near the bridge "the navel of the earth." Zinacantan is the center of the world, and Mexico City lies somewhere near the edge.

Mysticism and religious ceremonies, in combinations of ancient beliefs and Spanish Catholicism, permeate their lives. Baptism, courtship, marriage, housebuilding, illness, farming, and fiestas: Each has essential rituals to be observed. And in their deep-rooted wisdom the people and their rituals hold the universe and their role in it in delicate balance.

Mountains house ancestral gods; the "Earth Owner," an amoral and powerful *Ladino*, Spanish-speaking and non-Indian, lives underground with all his wealth. For many, the earth is still supported by four gods who can cause the earth to tremble as punishment to the people, or shift their burden when they tire, causing earthquakes that kill enough people to make their task easier.

"Our Holy Father" the sun travels a path that circles the world as does the moon, "Our Holy Mother." Stars light their way like candles as they pass below the earth through the lower world. This is shaped like an ancient Maya pyramid and occupied by a race of dwarfs who wear hats as protection against the heat. Fifty-five images of saints with extraordinary power and inner souls have homes in the churches and the houses of community leaders. Sacred crosses, decorated with pine branches and red geranium blossoms, mark mountains, water holes, and family compounds.

"When Zinacantecans light white wax candles at their mountain shrines," reports Evon Vogt, "they say they are offering 'tortillas' to their ancestral gods who live inside the mountains. They provide 'cigarettes' in the form of smoke from burning copal incense. Cane liquor, poured on the ground, completes the meal."

These ancestors are the models on which the people base their lives, and a man reaches high honor by officiating for one year in each of the four levels of *cargo*, or religious service. He must move into the central village and bear the financial burden of ceremonies. He is identified with a saint and assumes that saint's name. Then he returns to his hamlet to work his land and save enough money for another year of cargo at some time in the future.

Civil officials also serve in rotation, in jobs that vary from mayor and judges to policemen and errand boys. Their duties include public works, settling local disputes, and appointing committees to plan fiestas. The cargo system and civic offices control religious activities and serve the town well, but cannot assure its day-to-day livelihood.

After the Spanish Conquest, most Indian land gradually passed into the hands of the Ladinos and remained there until after the Mexican Revolution of 1910. Although little was returned before 1940, Zinacantecans have now regained 68 percent of their ancestral property. Many of these fields are owned by the community, and rights to them are assigned through a system called *ejido*. The Mexican government encourages Indians to become literate in Spanish, but I discovered a literacy program of another kind in Zinacantan.

Anthropologist John Burstein, formerly of the Harvard Project, has established a program to teach the people to read, write, and publish in their own language, which is Tzotzil Maya.

"This is their first publication," John told me proudly, and showed me a book by two men of Zinacantan. These talented and devoted authors are Chep Kontzarez and Manvel Hernandez. "They interviewed men and women, and plan to write their own history as it has been told to them: personal memories, genealogies, folk tales. There is a strong oral tradition here. We want to teach the women and children, but so far only the men have come to class."

It is easy for me to picture a highland Maya family sitting around the fire at night. I have shared such evenings in Yucatán with parents telling children old tales of family history so they will be proud of who they are. Making dark young eyes widen with stories of spirits and witches in the night. Amusing relatives of every age with tongue twisters, riddles, and jokes that are invariably bawdy and beyond translation with their puns.

Both in the highlands and lowlands, Maya priests must know from memory many rounds of long prayers. While now infused with Christianity, their chants often come from generations long past. One prayer, of the many collected by Evon Vogt in Zinacantan, is part of the cycle for the year renewal ceremony. It is at once intense and restrained as Maya priests chant in unison:

These offerings are not piled high,
They are not heaped high,
It is only a small bit,
It is only a humble amount,
  But grant us thy divine pardon,
  Grant us thy divine forgiveness,
  Receive this humble spray of flowers,
  Receive this humble branch of pine,
  Receive this humble bit of incense,
  Receive this humble cloud of smoke . . .
Receive then: your holy sun has gone over
the hill,
  Your holy year has passed,
  Take this for the holy end of the year,
  Take this for the holy end of the day. . . .

Walter F. (Chip) Morris, Jr., travels the Chiapas highlands collecting hand-woven textiles for museums, and works with the Mexican government establishing weaving co-ops of Maya women.

I visited the hamlet of Nabenchauk with him to meet a master weaver, Xunka Tulan, and her family at their mountainside home. Xunka's oldest daughter sat in a corner of the family compound working at her backstrap loom. They showed us their latest products: a boy's tunic, two stoles, and a white wedding huipil for one of Chip's collections. With white chicken feathers spun into the weft threads and woven into the cloth, and bordered in bright colors, it was stunning.

In pre-Conquest times, weavers in both the Maya and Mexican areas made feathered cloth. Some authorities think that the bridal huipil of Zinacantan derives from the Aztec.

"If that's true," says Chip, "the Aztec influence could reflect trade before the Conquest—or, more probably, interchange between the Zinacantecans and the Aztec troops that came with the conquerors and settled in San Cristóbal." In any case, the feather weaving of Mesoamerica has been lost everywhere except in Zinacantan; Chip calls these prized white huipils the tradition's "only living remnant."

Many highland Maya women own no more than ten "best" huipils in a lifetime, all nearly identical. Each village has its own style of dress; and a woman who marries outside her village adopts the huipil of her new home. Her children will also follow the style of their father's town. In some areas, cheaper, mass-produced clothing is replacing the traditional garments.

"Usually," Chip told me, "a weaver's career is finished by the time she is 50 or 55 years old. Such delicate work ruins their eyes." Ceremonial cloaks or jackets or trousers for men, and huipils and skirts for women, can be quite elaborate, and the symbolism of their designs complex.

Chip showed me a huipil from the village of Magdalenas, more than 20 years old: "The woman who wove this is illiterate—and a genius. It is the most complicated symbolic weaving I have ever seen."

Symbols on the front and back explain the weaver's position in her community and the cosmos. The sleeves show the relationship of such important figures as the rain god and the earth lord to the fertility of the land. Chip has learned to "read" the design, including small dots of color, and to analyze the mystical numerology.

"The weaver has created a huipil which describes the whole universe in a way so subtle that even fellow weavers won't notice, but so repetitious that the gods cannot help but see. She has described the complex relationship of time and space, and placed the gods of fertility in positions of power in order that all life may flourish. Wearing this huipil she becomes one of the daughters of the rain god; fearful of lightning, yet praying for rain."

Often as I have been in Yucatán, I made my first trip to the Chiapas highlands only recently. A village there is spectacular at first sight on any day, with all its citizens dressed alike in dramatic color; at fiesta time it can be breathtaking. As John Burstein told me, "The fiesta brings highland Maya culture to an artistic peak."

During Carnaval, just before Lent, George and I visited Tenejapa, near Zinacantan but differing in ritual details. We rounded a tall mountain on a bumpy dirt road and stopped the car in its tracks. There, in the village far below, a mass of people in red, white, and black packed the narrow streets. At opposite ends of town, two groups of men dressed in bright red costumes ran in meandering patterns while waving bright red banners. These costumes stem from the vestments of bishops, though the wearers are called *capitanes*.

We spent the morning in the village square watching one group of these "captains" swirl past as they ran behind a man encased in the straw effigy of a bull. Boys ran beside the bull flinging lassos at its

Studying aerial views, Sylvia Garza de González, director of the Yucatán Atlas Project, confers with her colleague and husband, Norberto González Crespo, regional director for the National Institute of Anthropology and History. By helicopter and light plane, they and their crews have surveyed nearly all the state of Yucatán. They consult satellite imagery as well, and make exhaustive checks for ground truth. Already they have located more than 1,000 pre-Columbian sites; their work yields new data on ancient Maya settlement patterns.

N.G.S. PHOTOGRAPHER OTIS IMBODEN

horns while a trumpeter blared shrill notes, and a drummer beat a doleful rhythm. Many Tenejapans, fortified with cane liquor, jiggled a dance to the music of a loudspeaker or collapsed in the street.

But if Carnaval is an ultimate revelry, Holy Week is a religious passion, building in intensity toward Good Friday.

hamula, the municipality that borders Zinacantan, observes it with special fervor. Unlike Zinacantan, which has multiple deities and several churches, Chamula primarily worships the sun, "Our Father" or "Our Lord of the Sky," who is also Jesus Christ. A single church serves some 40,000 Chamulans.

My friend John Armstrong, of Guatemala City, remembers visiting that church in 1965. He was there in Holy Week, when cargo holders adorn the interior with flowers and candles, and had the unusual privilege of seeing the Good Friday ritual.

"The rites began early in the morning," said John. "I stood pressed against the back wall. Over the crowd, I could see a huge cross erected in front of the altar. Men began moving a catafalque, bearing a full-size statue of Christ, down the aisle, and women were wailing around it. People sat on the floor, wailing, praying over their white candles, and drinking cane liquor. The catafalque inched forward imperceptibly. By late morning it had reached the altar, but a large black drapery hid the figure of Christ.

"Promptly at noon the church bell rang and suddenly the black cloth was lowered to reveal Christ hanging on the cross.

"Everyone cried out and everyone was kneeling. If I'd had enough space I would have done the same. Nothing has ever had such an emotional impact on me."

Maya customs sometimes seem strange to us, but ours can be nothing less than bizarre to the Maya. A few days before our first Easter in Yucatán, Maria and Irene helped George and me dye eggs for our oldest son, George.

"Why are we doing this?" they asked.

"Because it's Easter," we answered.

There was a long silence.

"In Yucatán, Easter is a religious time," said one.

"It is in the United States, too."

I have thought about that conversation many times since.

While the people of both Chamula and Zinacantan spend much of their time fulfilling their religious obligations, these increasingly conflict with earning a living.

New laws returned much of their ancestral lands to these Indian communities. But in recent times population has increased and land has not. An average highland field produces crops for two or three years, then must lie fallow for six or seven before it can be replanted. Chamulans and Zinacantecans have looked to the lowlands, at least since 1550. There, in the fertile basin of the Grijalva River, Zinacantan farmers rent plots from Ladino landowners.

Chamula owns more land than Zinacantan, but its population is much larger and much denser. Artisans as well as farmers work hard there, producing such items as furniture, musical instruments, bootleg cane liquor, and ceremonial sandals to sell to other municipalities. Still, employment is scarce. Beginning in the 19th century, farmers have sometimes overplanted and sheep overgrazed their pastures. A denuded hill slowly eroding into a valley is not an unusual sight. Most Chamula men must leave their village and become, temporarily, lowland plantation workers.

The Ladinos of highland Chiapas, although outnumbered by some seven to one, still control commerce, as they have since early colonial times. And their vast landholdings operate on Indian labor.

"Sometimes whole Indian families leave their villages for months at a time, but usually it is only the men who go," John Burstein told me. "And their absence is difficult for the women and children left behind."

In dealing with the Ladinos, the highland Maya show a notable tenacity. If necessary, they return to an office day after day and wait hour after hour to settle some commercial or legal matter. They show individuality as well. Recently, when the Mexican government put a television tower on Tzontehuitz, the sacred mountain of Chamula, anthropologists waited apprehensively for local reactions—and found they can't always predict them.

"Just look at what they've done," said Mol Komate, a village elder. "They built a beautiful tall silver sculpture up there and then topped it with a big red light!"

But not all of the surprises end so happily. For years, when Ladino plantation and ranch owners found themselves short of laborers, they employed a middleman—often called an *enganchador*, or hooker—to solicit workers. The enganchador took advantage of fiestas, when drinking is a ceremonial obligation. Many a man found in the reality of dawn that he had signed a contract the day before, or even had his signature forged; now a truck was taking him to the lowlands.

"In Chamula today, 90 percent of the men must work on fincas in the lowlands. Otherwise they would starve," John Burstein told me. "But they prefer to pick the time—and place." This is especially true of the cargo holder, whose duties demand his presence in Chamula and who dreads the shame of incurring onerous debt.

Priscilla R. Linn of the Harvard Project recorded a prayer in which the incoming cargo holder begs for divine help, because he is one

Who must not look for employment,
Who must not look for a weekly wage,
Who must not go to the fincas, father,
... not go to the rented lands. ...

uatemala offers variations of its own on the highland Maya theme, some as dramatic as the smoking volcanoes that loom above the restless deep waters of Lake Atitlán. Here also the highlands suffer from overpopulation; but some areas are pros-

perous, with farmers working the fertile land intensely and efficiently.

In a small valley near the town of Sololá, we spent part of a morning with farmers who till the rich volcanic soil. Irrigation ditches diverted cool water from mountain streams through carefully tended garden plots. Cabbages, potatoes, and garlic were ready for harvest in fields where I did not see a single weed. Other plots made a neat patchwork in shades of green across the small valley and up the terraced lower slopes of the surrounding mountains.

"Each family owns its farm," one man told me. "This is a good place. We feed ourselves and have plenty of vegetables to sell."

About 45 miles west of Lake Atitlán is the municipality of San Pedro Sacatepéquez. In the principal town, San Pedro, some 10,000 people make up one of the largest urban Indian concentrations in western Guatemala. Most are of Maya descent.

"It is one of the most productive and entrepreneurial towns in all of Guatemala," says anthropologist Waldemar Smith. "A center of commerce, trucking, and textile production, as well as the principal market for dozens of surrounding townships."

By Guatemalan standards, the Indians of San Pedro are well educated. Many have high-school diplomas or college degrees, and all show pride in their Indian background. Luxuries like cars, usually enjoyed only by Ladinos, are not unusual among them; many Indians are wealthy and live in houses much more elegant than those of their Ladino neighbors. Waldemar Smith describes one physician who considers the Spanish roots of some Guatemalans with wry humor, and his own heritage with pride.

"The doctor is a community leader," he says, "who keeps in his home, right above the bar, a 'coat of arms' emblazoned with a book and a hoe. These symbols, he says epitomize his origins."

Throughout the Guatemalan highlands, in tiny farming hamlets or thriving commercial towns, I was reminded of a national tragedy—the earthquake of February 1976. Bare wide gashes exposed the stone interior of mountains whose fields and forests had shaken loose and slid into the valley below. Hundreds of churches, jewels of colonial architecture, were totally destroyed or sagged hopelessly, their facades shored up by a few logs. Small adobe brick houses and their heavy wooden roof beams had collapsed by the thousand. Many Indians believe it was a punishment sent by God because of their sins. Whole villages were being rebuilt with lumber and tin; but more than a year and a half after the calamity, many families still lived in tents.

"It will take Guatemala ten more years to recover and finish rebuilding," a woman told me in Antigua. That city, built with Maya labor, was a colonial capital until the earthquakes of 1773 reduced it to rubble.

istorical patterns as well as natural ones have repeated themselves in Guatemala. Spanish conquerors found Maya cacao groves flourishing on the Pacific slopes and took them for their own, keeping the Indians as workers. Later the *fincas*, or plantations, grew sugar. About a century ago, coffee became a money crop. Today 70 percent of Guatemala's farmland belongs to plantation owners—and they comprise only 2 percent of all farm owners.

High on the fertile southern slope of Atitlán volcano, the finca of Los Andes resembles an enchanted garden at first sight. On a clear day the white plantation house has a sweeping view across its broad green lawn to the distant Pacific. Flowers bloom constantly in the perennial spring climate; breezes waft perfume from orange and allspice trees. The workers' small houses nestle close to the factory, or processing plant. There, the air is heavy with the scent of tea.

John Armstrong, a co-owner of the finca, welcomed us. "We began growing it several years ago. Now other fincas nearby also have tea," he explained. "All of it is processed here at Los Andes. We supply most of the tea consumed in Guatemala, but of course we also still grow coffee."

And quinine. And cardamom. Harvest means gathering a different part of each plant: beans from coffee, seeds from cardamom, bark from quinine, leaves from tea. Forty-three families live there permanently, tending and harvesting the major crops.

"They are of Indian descent, but they have been in this area so long they live and dress like Ladinos," said John. "In the four months when we work and harvest the coffee, migrant Indian families live here.

"There has been an amazing social change since tea harvesting began," he continued. "Women and children have more agile fingers than men. We pay by the pound, and often a child earns more than the father by picking tea. I call some of the children *maquinitas*—little machines, their hands go so fast. Whoever picks the most every day gets 25 cents extra."

That very day, two children had picked more than 100 pounds of tea—apiece. Raymond Irving-Bell, a junior partner, told us about it at dinner. It was a formidable accomplishment, for only the top two leaves and bud are picked from each branch.

Guatemala has set a minimum wage equal to $1.25 a day for agricultural workers, so plantation workers should average about $400 a year at best. I asked John and Raymond about the highland migrant workers at Los Andes.

"The highland families are very conservative," they told me. "There, too, we sometimes have problems. Men want their wives to stay at home and cook and weave, but many of the women say they want to earn extra money." *(Continued on page 189)*

(Continued on page 189)

Market day—Friday, in Sololá—brings Maya from outlying hamlets to the highland town to buy, sell, and trade. Some still carry their goods—avocados, onions, sandals, turkeys—by bundle and tumpline. And others now truck theirs to market.

Under a weighty sky, a boy of Sololá rolls his hoop along a bluff above Lake Atitlán. On the

steep, terraced slope behind him, his family and neighbors raise their supply of corn.

Faces impassive, garments eloquent, bystanders at the Sololá market observe a transaction—prudent bargaining over a few centavos. The stylized motif of a bat wing appears on the sleeves of their jackets; it proves them men of Sololá. Not only a hub of local trade, their town lies on a route between high country and low. Merchants taking the Pan American Highway will come here to sell tropical products such as spices, bananas, cocoa. They buy pottery and textiles for resale, and drive on. In late afternoon, a band sets out on the highway to perform in the next town. They carry drums, popular in antiquity; a bass fiddle, known since the Conquest; and a marimba. Of African provenance, the marimba came with slaves imported to fill the disease-thinned crews of Maya tribute labor.

Daybreak ritual completed, religious leaders of Chichicastenango descend the steps of the Church of Santo Tomás. Before its door they offer prayer and burn copal for incense. As always on occasions of duty, they wear red headdresses and black coats and carry sacred silver standards that the bare hand must not touch. After 400 years of Catholic influence, the Maya of highland Guatemala cherish ancient beliefs. They equate important days in the 260-day ritual calendar with dates sacred to Christians. Prayers invoke the Holy Trinity—and deities known to the Maya before the Spanish Conquest. On market day, a man in Ladino clothing places copal wrapped in cornhusks on a fire at the church steps. Each Sunday, this plaza comes alive, an endpoint to varying pilgrimages. Indians come to trade, but also make an offering at the steps.

Many finca owners pay the medical expenses of resident workers and their families, and Los Andes now has its own dispensary. This is a project of INCAP—the Institute for Nutrition for Central America and Panama, a regional center of the 75-year-old Pan American Health Organization which is now an agency of the United Nations. INCAP has begun a health program on five fincas, including Los Andes.

"They're learning the importance of boiling their drinking water, a balanced diet, and cleanliness in preparing their food," Raymond told me. "The results have been amazing. Before, the carpenter was often sawing lumber for a coffin. But now it has been ages since he made one. And INCAP is training a Los Andes girl to be a medical aide for the people here."

Some sixty miles to the west, John Graham is excavating the site of Abaj Takalik that spreads across four coffee fincas. These lie more or less on the border of present-day Mam and Quiché Maya.

"We employ both Mam and Quiché men at the dig," John told me. "The resident workers on the fincas were Indians; but now they think of themselves as Ladinos, and our Maya workmen agree. In fact, our crews call the residents 'foreigners' and refer to themselves as 'people.' "

Time never buried one of the ancient monuments. It sits partially exposed, showing a man holding a feline.

"The workmen say he's holding a rabbit. We find offerings of rum and candles in front of it at dawn," said John. "A giant snake is supposed to live in a cave nearby; people also leave offerings at the entrance. I've been told that a giant rabbit lives here

Apprenticed early, a little girl sits pensively in a pottery co-op in Amatenango, Chiapas. Here, at five or six, girls learn to make figurines and toy pots under their mothers' tutelage; after four or five years they begin making pots for kitchen use or for sale to tourists.

on the mound. He can be seen hopping around in the middle of the night."

At one of these fincas, San Isidro, the owner's wooden Victorian house sat high on top of an ancient mound.

"The owner isn't here. He only visits from time to time," the finca manager told us. "But would you like to see the old sculpture up in the garden?"

We followed him up the steep steps of the mound. In the garden, a potbellied Preclassic figure in stone sat in the shade of an orange tree.

To the east, forested mountains roll downward toward the Usumacinta River and its tributary the Lacantun. This name, corrupted to Lacandon, gave the Spaniards a designation for the Maya of the vicinity. The first "Lacandon" were Chol speakers, conquered in the 1690's and deported after 1712 to serve as laborers. The last of them died toward the end of the century, only a few miles from Abaj Takalik.

But long before the Chol Lacandon were defeated, other Maya were taking refuge in this low, hot jungle country. They filtered in from Tabasco, southern Campeche, Yucatán, and from across the Usumacinta. They hacked scattered farmsteads out of the forest and, until recently, changed little through the centuries. Their descendants are called Lacandon today.

James D. Nations of Southern Methodist University has lived with the Lacandon for 22 months. I met him in San Cristóbal de Las Casas, and he gave me an up-to-date account of their condition.

"For years," he said, "anthropologists have thought the Lacandon were almost extinct. But that isn't true now. They're increasing. There are about 350 of them, living in seven villages."

The Mexican government has brought them from isolated farms into these seven communities for better control. While population increases, so does contact with outsiders; and communicable diseases abound. As so often with the Maya, new circumstances only repeat old patterns.

The Lacandon forest is rich with mahogany and cedar. Since 1871, the government has run logging operations there, and in the past few years Indians have been paid for the timber taken from their land.

"Seventy percent of the lumber money is put into community funds. The rest is paid to heads of families in cash," said Jim. "The Lacandon do not fully understand why they receive this money, and some refer to those who bring it to them as 'the men who give away money.'"

Recently this rich terrain has attracted other groups. Much of the northern forest has been cleared for grassland on cattle ranches owned by both Ladinos and Indians. About 12,000 other Maya have migrated into the area—most of them Tzeltal and Chol. The government has placed them into two new settlements. They, too, receive lumber royalties, but the money is divided evenly among the three groups: a third for several thousand Tzeltales, a third for several thousand Chol, a third for a few hundred Lacandon. Many Chol and Tzeltales feel themselves short-changed; and some, under cover of night, have begun to slip away.

Lacandon still farm, growing a surprising variety of vegetables and fruits. But as with all the Maya, corn is the cherished staple of their diet. They fell tall mahoganies and cedars to carve dugout canoes, and fish in the blue lagoons and wide sluggish rivers. Game, like deer and peccary, is plentiful in the jungle.

Hach uinik, they call themselves, "true people." In the shelter of their thatched "god houses" they pray to ancient deities and practice sacred rites that reach back through uncounted generations. Copal incense flames in clay "god pots." Balché ferments in a ceremonial canoe. Voices rise in prayers for rain, to cure illness, or, more rarely, to free the sun from an eclipse.

Deities of a great pantheon vary in name and importance from one Lacandon group to another. To some, Mensabak, the rain god, holds greater sway, while others place the sun, K'in, in supreme power. Souls of their ancestors live in the ruins of Yaxchilán, nearby. They travel there to pray and bring back a stone to put in the clay pots that represent gods.

Bark paper, made by the ancient Maya for their codices, is still made the same way, pounded smooth with wooden beaters. Lacandon dye it red with annatto seeds, cut it into strips to make ritual headbands, or cut notches on the bottom to represent individual deities and hang them in their god houses.

In recent years missionaries have converted some Lacandon to fundamentalist Protestantism, but all remain a blend of traditional and new, adapting in their own way to the world around them. Increased contact with the outside world has introduced new elements.

"It can be quite startling," said Jim, "to round a bend on a jungle path and meet a Lacandon wearing pink polyester pants under his white tunic and holding a transistor radio pressed to one ear."

A taxi arrived in San Cristóbal during our visit. Chan K'in—Little Sun, 16-year-old son and namesake of a Lacandon chief—had come from the airport with his 15-year-old wife, Nuk. The taxi's trunk stood agape, bristling with bows and hundreds of arrows they had brought to sell to tourists. Chan K'in wore his tunic with shiny black plastic Wellington boots; Nuk had tucked her tunic into a red plaid skirt.

I bought a pottery drum from him to keep near my desk, a molded face on one side upturned and open-mouthed. It is the Lacandon singing god, K'ayum.

Especially at death, customs from ancient times prevail. Only a few years ago, anthropologists reported that a Lacandon is buried with a gourd of corn gruel for his journey through the underworld, a bit of hair for the louse he will meet, corn for a hen that might frighten him, and a bone for the dog that will carry him across the river of tears. In a small carving of incised bone from a tomb at Tikal, the tomb of Double-Comb, a small creature that may be such a dog shares a canoe voyage with the departed through wildly surging waters.

With transistor radios and polyester fashions as much a part of their everyday lives as incense and ancient gods, Jim Nations borrows an image from a colleague to prophesy their future: "Lacandon society will be a new culture . . . retaining only a few anachronistic cultural traits which persist like a watch ticking in the pocket of a dead man."

Time was their obsession. Change has been their story. The Maya, in their long journey from mysterious beginnings to their role in the modern world, have been a dynamic presence. In almost twenty years—a mere katun—I have glimpsed a segment of time, a period of alteration in Yucatán.

When we lived at Cobá we returned to Mérida frequently and visited with friends. Tránsita and her aunt, Modesta, gave Ann and me embroidery lessons. They showed us how to draw threads from white cloth for openwork, and make half-forgotten designs in vivid thread. We spent several afternoons with them, gossiping and joking and trying to master the complex work that seemed so easy for them.

"Girls today don't want to do hand embroidery," complained Tránsita. "They wear huipils made by machine. When I was young, girls stayed home, but now they want to go all the time. Always in the streets, going somewhere.

"We had a big fiesta every year in Telchaquillo and every year we girls made a new huipil for it. The day after the fiesta we would start making a new one. It took that long.

"My papa would buy the cloth and the colors of thread we wanted, and then he would say, 'Now I've done my part. The rest is up to you.'

"Many nights my sisters and I got up at

About two feet tall and nearly as wide, a very fat piggy bank waits to go to market— for the tourist trade in Mérida. The work of a Maya potter, José Augusto Pech, its cheerful paint and expansive presence speak for a side of the Maya character not always obvious: an earthy sense of fun that finds satisfaction in puns and riddles and jokes.

two in the morning and sat around a little table with one candle, whispering and giggling and embroidering until dawn."

She laughed and shook her head. "Now always in the streets. Everything by machine."

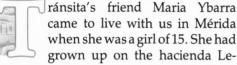Tránsita's friend Maria Ybarra came to live with us in Mérida when she was a girl of 15. She had grown up on the hacienda Lepán, owned then by a member of the Peón family. Her mother is Maya; her father was a Korean sent to Yucatán as a child laborer before the turn of the century, and given a Spanish name.

Maria learned Catholicism in the hacienda chapel, Maya rituals and stories from her mother and elderly godparents who lived on a ranch nearby. Maya was her first language, and the Spanish that she knew she taught me—with a Maya accent.

Now she is a Mérida matron, married to a skilled stonemason, and the mother of five. Her Spanish is perfect. She speaks Maya occasionally but her husband, Jorge Flores, and the children do not speak it at all. The family has converted to the Mormon faith. They are an urban family—part of Mexico's expanding middle class.

On our latest visit to Mérida, we spent several evenings with them, enjoying the cool patio while the children watched television inside. The family motorcycle was parked nearby.

"The house is paid for," said Jorge; "I'm planning to build a second story."

They told us of trips to Mexico City. Maria and some of the children planned a visit to the new beach resort of Cancún in Quintana Roo.

She spent an afternoon retelling me old tales, ceremonies and cures that she had learned as a child from her relatives and godparents. But that young girl who embroidered huipils and made a hetzmek ceremony for our son so many years ago was now living in another world.

Change has come with comparable speed to Cobá, a new village in the ruins of an ancient city. About twenty years ago, settlers came from older villages in the state of Yucatán to ring the shore of Lake Cobá with their pole-and-thatch houses and start a new life for themselves.

Mexico has encouraged settlers to come into Quintana Roo. Stronghold of Maya rebels in the War of the Castes, it is still the least populated of all the states in Mexico. Until 1974, it had remained a federal territory. Land there is free for the taking and settling, but only those hardy souls with frontier spirit remain to carve the thorn scrub into milpas and ranches.

Our house sat on an ancient platform beside the lake. The floor was earth; the walls were slender trees bound together with vines; the roof was leaves—nature gently rearranged into shelter.

Don Sabino was the first villager I met in Cobá. He is one of the few old men there, and lives across the lake. We had arrived late one night, and early next morning he came to pay a call—to welcome me. We could chat quite well in Spanish, but he insisted on teaching me Maya and set about it immediately. We sat on the log stoop, and he pointed and told me words: house, lake, sky, sun, horse.

He asked me words in English, pointing too. He mispronounced them, tried again, wrinkling up his wrinkled face. He pointed to the sun and I told him, "sun," then to Greg and I told him, "son."

"Lo mismo? Que bonito. Bonito.—The same? How beautiful. Beautiful."

I was to see him often in the next two summers, bringing watermelons or sour oranges from his milpa to sell, or leading his horse laden with bags of cement to the spot where Mexican archeologists were reconstructing a temple.

Once, when I shouted for help, Don Sabino answered. But, always polite, he shook hands, smiled, and asked about the children's health before killing the green tree viper that hung just over my head in the thatch.

First settlers and newcomers alike, people of the village own the land communally, and their fields are parceled out by the ejido leaders. Many villagers own cattle that forage in the jungle, and some have moved out to start their own ranches miles away from Cobá.

"Too many people in that village. I had to get away," said one rancher. There are just over a hundred settlers.

Almost half of them now attend the little mission church across the lake from our house. Many nights we lay in our hammocks listening to Maya voices sing Protestant hymns in Spanish. The minister always preached through a bull horn, making certain that his words fell on Catholic ears as well.

Those who have remained Catholic are the ones who still perform the old ceremonies: corn planting, hetzmek, Chachaac. The Maya priest who performed the Chachaac ceremony that I attended felt certain that Chaac did not really approve of the minister and his bull horn.

In a large group of ruined temples at one end of the lake, part of a stela still stands at the base of a tall pyramid that local Maya call *la iglesia*—the church. The stela's surface is so badly eroded that the carved glyphs and headdress on it are hardly discernible. Some call it a king of Cobá; others say it is an ancient goddess.

Ann found her friend Amelia there one afternoon with her family and friends. They invited Ann to join them. Amelia's wedding was only a few days away, and she was leaving to live in Yucatán. The women wore their best huipils with thin shawls slung from their arms like small silk hammocks. Five beeswax candles burned at the stela base; gourds of zacá sat in front. There were prayers and songs, and everyone drank a gourd of zacá.

I have often seen candles there, and sometimes an offering of food. In the hours just before dawn, men of Cobá set out with their dogs to hunt deer deep in the jungle, but first they stop a moment

Holding a sprig of flowers, a Maya boy of Yucatán plays on the wheel of a machine that once spun a hacienda's henequen into rope but now lies idle. The industry, reformed by law in 1937, limps along, prey to an uncertain and increasingly competitive world market. The boy, learning Spanish in school, may find some new employment, ever more remote from the ways of the past.

NATIONAL GEOGRAPHIC PHOTOGRAPHER OTIS IMBODEN

to pray and give a candle to the goddess. These ruins are bringing the whole of the outside world into this small farming community, for there seems to be a growing curiosity about the ancient Maya. At first just a few tourists came each week, bumping along the unpaved narrow lane. Now tour buses arrive frequently on the wide new highway. We have heard of plans for a hotel at Cobá. Some of our Maya friends have opened refreshment stands, and planned to open restaurants.

From their earliest prehistory until today, each generation of the Maya people has seen new ideas, change, movement. The past in ancient belief *is* the present and future, forever repeating; and that truth occurred to me repeatedly in my search for the modern Maya and their ancestral ties.

I talked with Waldemar Smith about the Maya and their history of conquest, rebellions, and displacement.

"Unfortunately, theirs has frequently been a story of exploitation. Remember that," he said. "And their role now is a vital part of our varied modern world. Be sure to remember that, too."

I thought of our visit to San Isidro, one of the fincas at Abaj Takalik. I had sat on the shady porch of what was once the office-and-company-store. I could imagine the workers of a century ago, standing in line before the screened window of the paymaster, carefully counting their *centavos* and wondering if they would be able to reduce their debt to the owner, at least a little. And then going inside to buy food, and perhaps a few other essentials like a needle and a length of thread.

Today that building is the manager's office and nothing more. Buses take the workers of San Isidro to nearby towns for their shopping.

I had gazed across the dusty road as people clambered into a truck, on their way to plant new trees. Each one carried tin cans with coffee seedlings. Some of the women wore dresses; others, the dark skirts and brocaded blouses of highland Indians.

"A picture of the Maya today would show every shade of traditional and modern living," Bob Carmack said to me.

I have seen it many times. With conscious pride, stonemasons of Oxkutzcab in Yucatán, who reconstruct the ruined cities, have built their town a train station in the shape of a Maya temple. A physician with a Maya name, Luna Kan, governs their state. A Maya village, Chemax, has elected a woman mayor, *Alcaldesa* Marciela Diaz Castellanos. In highland Guatemala, Quiché elders calculate with the old 260-day calendar, anxious to know if New Year's Day, the Year Bearer, bodes good or evil. My friend Maria Ybarra tells me none of her children has had the hetzmek ceremony. In Zinacantan a man looks forward to his first year of religious cargo, the burden he will assume as his merchant ancestors took bundles through the highlands—or as a Classic glyph bears a segment of time.

Archeological scholarship may enjoy a renaissance if recent interpretations and glyph translations are correct. Far southwest of Cobá, the great ruler Pacal lies in his splendid tomb at Palenque. The arrangement of figures and symbols around his sarcophagus has caused much perplexity, but Linda Schele believes the difficulty has been in the viewer.

"They were arranged for *Pacal* to consider, not for someone outside the sarcophagus," she told me. "When you think of him as the focal point it becomes clear. He is surrounded by his ancestors and will always be in their center—in the center of his universe."

I remembered Chip Morris's "huipil of genius" from the highlands.

"Linda, that same principle appears in modern weaving!" And we compared notes with astonishment and satisfaction: an ancient ruler established in eternity, a living woman walking a highland path wearing symbols that are a silent conversation with the rain god.

I have often walked the limestone roads of Cobá, the hot dusty new ones and the rubble of the ancient ones. I have taken a path newly slashed through the jungle, thinking of our work and its setting.

We in archeology always remained a group within a group at Cobá, bound together by nature as it swirled around us in accelerated patterns of life, reproduction, and death.

Vines twirling around trees and choking them. Trees thrusting upward for light and straining their roots down into the dry limestone for moisture.

Frogs, lizards, snakes, turtles—seeking to eat and go on eating one another and the insects. Large and solitary insects, or smaller ones by the swarm or hive, buzzing or marching through their cycle. Hornets stinging grasshoppers. Army ants moving on a wasp nest, passing the eggs over their shiny crisp bodies down the line in unthinking predisposed organization.

Under this: Under all these layers of life lie the ruins. Layers so packed together that when a tree dies it is not given the dignity of falling, but is held upright in the thickening vines as a lair or food or support for living things.

But this was a city of living people, its smooth causeways buzzing with travelers as they hurried past breadnut trees and neat garden plots on the outskirts, past the blue lakes toward tall groups of temples red in the brilliant sun. Now we may know the name of one of those people, a child who lived here more than a thousand years ago.

A broken limestone slab was found in the rubble of a collapsed building in 1974. It is unique as far as we know, for glyphs inscribed on its top follow the rectangular edge and then turn inward into a spiral. The carving has suffered from erosion, but some glyphs have, tentatively, been translated: Death . . . Smoking Mirror . . . [who was the child of] Lady MaCuc [and] the child of Lord . . . of Cobá. . . .

The remainder is still undeciphered.

The stone was probably a sarcophagus cover. It is small, small enough for a child. And only a child of the nobility would have been honored with such a burial. The mother shares the name Cuc, or Squirrel, with a powerful ruler of Naranjo, the Lord Zic Cuc, known as Smoking Squirrel. It is he whose marriage to a lady of Tikal, on August 28, 682, is recorded on monuments at both Cobá and Naranjo, 250 miles apart.

Who then was Smoking Mirror? The child of a ruler? Were the rulers of Cobá and Naranjo related, or allied by marriage? Did Smoking Mirror die before his time? And had he lived, would he have ruled a powerful city? Did the fortunes of a dynasty change at a princeling's death?

The glyphs are carved so that we had to walk around the stone counterclockwise several times to see them properly. It reminded me of a hetzmek ceremony; the slab, of a tabletop. Did priests and Smoking Mirror's noble kin walk these same rounds many centuries ago—perhaps as part of a ceremony for his future, an aid to his journey through the Underworld?

And how soon after his death was he forgotten, or so unimportant that part of his tomb was used as building stone?

No one knows his story.

One morning at first light, just as birds began to sing and things unseen began to hum, I stood in a Classic Maya patio at Cobá, knee-deep in undergrowth. The buildings around it probably served as residences and temples for the elite, for they are set apart, and the patio opens onto a lake. But now jungle has reclaimed it. A cool breeze rippled across the lake and set trees and vines asway. I touched a temple wall beside me where a patch of smooth plaster still clung. On it, the graceful black lines of painted glyphs were barely visible. A toucan, almost half his length a yellow beak, glided slowly from one treetop to another. I stood perfectly still, listening, looking, and for a fleeting moment felt that I belonged there with him.

Acknowledgments

The Special Publications Division acknowledges with pleasure the hospitality and many kindnesses of the Instituto de Antropología e Historia of Guatemala; and of the Instituto Nacional de Antropología e Historia of Mexico, and the Museo Nacional de Antropología in Mexico City. The Division is equally grateful to collectors who wish to remain anonymous, to the individuals and organizations named or quoted in the text, and to those cited here for their generous cooperation and assistance during the preparation of this book: the Duke University Museum of Art; Dumbarton Oaks Research Library and Collections; the Middle American Research Institute, Tulane University; the Pre-Columbian Art Research Center, Palenque; the Science Museum of Minnesota, St. Paul; and Anthony Andrews, Joann M. Andrews, Thomas Bolt, William Brito Sansores, Donald L. and Lolita Brockington, Persis B. Clarkson, Peter Gullotti, Richard and Anita Hedlund, Nicholas M. Hellmuth, Leticia Rozo Krauss, Robert M. Laughlin, Luis Lujan Muñoz, Christopher Lutz, Sidney D. Markman, Francisco Peón Ancona, Luis Ramírez Aznar, Eric von Euw, Robert Wasserstrom.

Drawings for illuminated letters and for chapter devices by George E. Stuart. Glyphs from various carvings in the corpus of Maya inscriptions. Jaguar-motif devices: Chapter 1: Olmec were-jaguar. Chapter 2: Late Preclassic stucco mask, structure E-VII-sub, Uaxactún. Chapter 3: Stone mosaic mask, Palace of the Masks, Kabah. Chapter 4: Colonial street marker, stone bas-relief, Mérida. Chapter 5: Contemporary dance mask, wood and papier-mâché, Suchiapa, Chiapas.

Authors' Note

To the writing of this book the Stuarts bring more than twenty years' experience and expertise in archeology.

Both grew up in South Carolina—Gene in Anderson, George in Camden—and both earned bachelor's degrees at the University of South Carolina, Gene in art and English, George in geology. They met in 1954 while working at Etowah Mounds in Georgia and were married that same year; they have four children, and now make their home in Chapel Hill, North Carolina. Their collaborative works include the Society's annotated anthropological map Indians of North America and the Special Publication *Discovering Man's Past in the Americas*.

Skilled in restoring and rendering ceramics, Gene has taught art at the high-school and college level. She served as staff artist during the excavation of the Maya ruins at Dzibilchaltún, illustrated Tulane's site report *Balankanche, Throne of the Tiger Priest*, and is currently drawing the murals of the Pinturas group of ruins at Cobá. Her free-lance publications include educational filmstrips and a children's book, *Three Little Indians*, for Special Publications.

George joined the Society's cartographic staff in 1960 and now serves as the Society's staff archeologist. He received his master's degree in anthropology from George Washington University, his Ph.D. from the University of North Carolina. He has taught at George Washington and at Catholic University, and given lectures at the Smithsonian Institution. His publications for the Society include a noteworthy article on progress in deciphering Maya glyphs in the December 1975 NATIONAL GEOGRAPHIC; and in 1976 he wrote a guide to professional study, *Your Career in Archaeology*, published for high-school and college students by the Society for American Archaeology.

Additional Reading

The reader may want to check the *National Geographic Index* for related material; the Society has published many articles on archeology in Mesoamerica from March 1913, when Sylvanus G. Morley reported excavations at Quiriguá, to December 1975, with four articles on the Maya.

The reader may also wish to consult the Society's Archeological Map of Middle America, researched and compiled by Dr. Stuart, and the Special Publication *Discovering Man's Past in the Americas*.

The following may also be useful:

Works spanning prehistory, historic, and contemporary material: Robert Wauchope, ed., *Handbook of Middle American Indians*, vols. 2, 3, 4, 6, 7; Eric Wolf, *Sons of the Shaking Earth*.

Books stressing archeology: George F. Andrews, *Maya Cities*; Richard E. W. Adams, *Prehistoric Mesoamerica*, ed., *The Rise of Maya Civilization*; Elizabeth P. Benson, *The Maya World*; Heinrich Berlin, *Signos y significados en las inscripciones mayas*; Michael D. Coe, *The Maya, The Maya Scribe and His World*; T. Patrick Culbert, *The Lost Civilization: The Story of the Classic Maya*, ed., *The Classic Maya Collapse*; David H. Kelley, *Deciphering the Maya Script*; Tatiana Proskouriakoff, *An Album of Maya Architecture*; Alberto Ruz Lhuillier, *Costumbres funerarias de los antiguas mayas*; George I. Sánchez, *Arithmetic in Maya*; J. Eric S. Thompson, *Maya Archaeologist, Maya History and Religion, The Rise and Fall of Maya Civilization*; Robert Wauchope, *Lost Tribes and Sunken Continents, They Found the Buried Cities*.

Books stressing the Spanish Conquest, the historic period, or contemporary life: Ruth Bunzel, *Chichicastenango*; Robert Carmack, *Quichean Civilization*; Robert Chamberlain, *The Conquest and Colonization of Yucatan*; Patricia de Fuentes, ed., *The Conquistadors*; Munro S. Edmondson, *The Book of Counsel: the Popol Vuh of the Quiché Maya of Guatemala*; Diego de Landa, *Relation of the Things of Yucatán*, ed. A. R. Pagden (1975), ed. Alfred M. Tozzer (1941); Murdo J. MacLeod, *Spanish Central America*; June Nash, *In the Eyes of the Ancestors*; Manning Nash, *Machine Age Maya*; Carmen L. Pettersen, *The Maya of Guatemala*; Adrián Recinos and Delia Goetz, *The Annals of the Cakchiquels*; Robert Redfield, *The Folk Culture of Yucatan*; Nelson Reed, *The Caste War of Yucatan*; Ralph Roys, *The Indian Background of Colonial Yucatan*, ed., *The Book of Chilam Balam of Chumayel*; Demetrio Sodi Morales, *The Maya World*; John L. Stephens, *Incidents of Travel in Central America, Chiapas and Yucatan, Incidents of Travel in Yucatan*; Evon Z. Vogt, *Zinacantan: A Maya Community in the Highlands of Chiapas*; Carter Wilson, *Crazy February*.

Index

A Note on Pronunciation and Spelling

Vowels in Maya words usually take the sounds ah, ay, ee, oh, and oo, while x corresponds to the English "sh." Words are generally accented on the final syllable. Some examples follow:

Chemax = chay MAHSH. Uxmal = oosh MAHL. Oxkutzcab = ohsh kootz KAHB. Dzibilchaltún = tseeb eel chahl TOON. Yaxchilán = yahsh chee LAHN. Transcription of Maya place-names and personal names often follows Spanish spelling and pronunciation. Some examples:

Kaminaljuyú = kah mee nahl hoo YOO. Jaina = HIGH na.

The Maya word *ahau,* meaning "lord," has survived as a surname and often appears as such with the spelling "Ajau." Spanish scholars, however, often use the spelling "Ahau" in referring to the Maya sun god or day name. Both spellings are pronounced "ah HOW."

Moreover, Maya renderings of foreign words may introduce other variations, such as "Tunatiuh" for the Nahuatl "Tonatiuh" or "Manvel" for the Spanish "Manuel." As a result, complete consistency is impossible; this book follows established usage in general but individual preference for personal names.

Library of Congress CIP Data

Stuart, George E
  The mysterious Maya.

  Bibliography: p.196.
  Includes index.
  1. Mayas. I. Stuart, Gene S., joint author. II. National Geographic Society, Washington, D. C. Special Publications Division. III. Title.
F1435.S89   970'.004'97   76-52648
ISBN 0-87044-233-3

Composition for *The Mysterious Maya* by National Geographic's Photographic Services, Carl M. Shrader, Chief; Lawrence F. Ludwig, Assistant Chief. Printed and bound by Kingsport Press, Kingsport, Tenn. Color separations by Colorgraphics, Inc., Forestville, Md.; Graphic South, Charlotte, N.C.; National Bickford Graphics, Inc., Providence, R.I.; Progressive Color Corp., Rockville, Md.; J. Wm. Reed Co., Alexandria, Va.